HENDERSON LIBRARIES

3 1431 00627 1340

W9-AAE-271

Henderson Libraries
280 S. Green Valley Pkwy
Henderson, NV 89012
702-492-7252

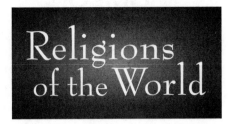

Religions
of the World

Sikhism

Nancy Hoffman

LUCENT BOOKS

An imprint of Thomson Gale, a part of The Thomson Corporation

THOMSON

GALE

Detroit • New York • San Francisco • San Diego • New Haven, Conn. • Waterville, Maine • London • Munich

© 2006 Thomson Gale, a part of The Thomson Corporation.

Thomson and Star Logo are trademarks and Gale and Lucent Books are registered trademarks used herein under license.

For more information, contact
Lucent Books
27500 Drake Rd.
Farmington Hills, MI 48331-3535
Or you can visit our Internet site at http://www.gale.com

ALL RIGHTS RESERVED.
No part of this work covered by the copyright hereon may be reproduced or used in any form or by any means—graphic, electronic, or mechanical, including photocopying, recording, taping, Web distribution, or information storage retrieval systems—without the written permission of the publisher.

Every effort has been made to trace the owners of copyrighted material.

LIBRARY OF CONGRESS CATALOGING-IN-PUBLICATION DATA

Hoffman, Nancy, 1955–
    Sikhism / by Nancy Hoffman.
    p. cm. — (Religions of the world)
    Includes bibliographical references and index.
    ISBN 1-59018-453-X (hard cover : alk. paper)
    1. Sikhism—History. 2. Sikhism—Customs and practices. 3. Sikhism and politics.
    I. Title. II. Series: Religions of the world (San Diego, Calif.)
    BL2017.6.H64 2005
    294.6—dc22
                                                              2004020782

Printed in the United States of America

Contents

Foreword

Religion has always been a central component of human culture, though its form and practice have changed through time. Ancient people lived in a world they could not explain or comprehend. Their world consisted of an environment controlled by vague and mysterious powers attributed to a wide array of gods. Artifacts dating to a time before recorded history suggest that the religion of the distant past reflected this world, consisting mainly of rituals devised to influence events under the control of these gods.

The steady advancement of human societies brought about changes in religion as in all other things. Through time, religion came to be seen as a system of beliefs and practices that gave meaning to—or allowed acceptance of—anything that transcended the natural or the known. And, the belief in many gods ultimately was replaced in many cultures by the belief in a Supreme Being.

As in the distant past, however, religion still provides answers to timeless questions: How, why, and by whom was the universe created? What is the ultimate meaning of human life? Why is life inevitably followed by death? Does the human soul continue to exist after death, and if so, in what form? Why is there pain and suffering in the world, and why is there evil?

In addition, all the major world religions provide their followers with a concrete and clearly stated ethical code. They offer a set of moral instructions, defining virtue and evil and what is required to achieve goodness. One of these universal moral codes is compassion toward others above all else. Thus, Judaism, Christianity, Islam, Hinduism, Buddhism, Confucianism, and Taoism each teach a version of the so-called golden rule, or in the words of Jesus Christ, "As ye would that men should do to you, do ye also to them likewise" (Luke 6:31). For example, Confucius instructed his disciples to "never impose on others what you would not choose for yourself" (*Analects:* 12:2). The Hindu epic poem,

Mahabharata, identifies the core of all Hindu teaching as not doing unto others what you do not wish done to yourself. Similarly Muhammad declared that no Muslim could be a true believer unless he desires for his brother no less than that which he desires for himself.

It is ironic, then, that although compassionate concern for others forms the heart of all the major religions' moral teachings, religion has also been at the root of countless conflicts throughout history. It has been suggested that much of the appeal that religions hold for humankind lies in their unswerving faith in the truth of their particular vision. Throughout history, most religions have shared a profound confidence that their interpretation of life, God, and the universe is the right one, thus giving their followers a sense of certainty in an uncertain and often fragile existence. Given the assurance displayed by most religions regarding the fundamental correctness of their teachings and practices, it is perhaps not surprising that religious intolerance has fueled disputes and even full-scale wars between peoples and nations time and time again, from the Crusades of medieval times to the current bloodshed in Northern Ireland and the Middle East.

Today, as violent religious conflicts trouble many parts of our world, it has become more important than ever to learn about the similarities as well as the differences between faiths. One of the most effective ways to accomplish this is by examining the beliefs, customs, and values of various religions. In the Religions of the World series, students will find a clear description of the core creeds, rituals, ethical teachings, and sacred texts of the world's major religions. In-depth explorations of how these faiths changed over time, how they have influenced the social customs, laws, and education of the countries in which they are practiced, and the particular challenges each one faces in coming years are also featured.

Extensive quotations from primary source materials, especially the core scriptures of each faith, and a generous number of secondary source quotations from the works of respected modern scholars are included in each volume in the series. It is hoped that by gaining insight into the faiths of other peoples and nations, students will not only gain a deeper appreciation and respect for different religious beliefs and practices, but will also gain new perspectives on and understanding of their own religious traditions.

Who Are the Sikhs?

Founded only five hundred years ago, Sikhism has grown to become the fifth largest religion in the world. Today there are approximately 23 million Sikhs worldwide, the majority of whom live in the Punjab region of India, where the faith was founded. Sikhism has also spread to Europe, North America, Australia, and Africa despite the fact that it rejects the concept of converting others. Sikhism's rapid growth in a relatively short period of time can be attributed to the culturally diverse region of its origin; its simple and progressive teachings, which stress equality among all religions, men and women, and rich and poor; and its tradition of helping those in need.

The Sikh faith is based on the philosophies and practices developed by ten gurus, or holy teachers. Sikhism's founder and first guru, Nanak, was influenced by the teachings of Islam and Hinduism, which thrived in the Punjab during his lifetime. Nanak's philosophy appealed to many Muslims and Hindus of his era because it was familiar and because it seemed more welcoming—it encouraged greater religious and social tolerance. While similar to Hinduism and Islam, Sikh philosophy under the first guru required simple expressions of faith not through collective ritual and religious customs as much as through individual daily prayer, meditation, and community service. Those practices serve a single

The turbans this man and his young son wear are visible signs of their adherence to the Sikh faith.

goal—total devotion to God, the Divine Creator. The Mul Mantra, one of the basic prayers Sikhs recite every day, honors and defines God according to the teachings of Sikhism. One of many slightly varying translations of the Mul Mantra simply states:

One Universal Creator God.
The Name is Truth.
Creative Being Personified.
No Fear, No Hatred.
Image of the Undying,

Beyond Birth, Self-Existent.
By Guru's Grace.[1]

For Sikhs, service to humankind is an important form of devotion to God. Nanak and the Sikh leaders who followed him encouraged—even required—all Sikhs to help others by cooking and serving meals to the hungry, ministering to the sick, and otherwise volunteering in their communities. The good will such service created helped spread the Sikh faith.

Size of Major World Religions

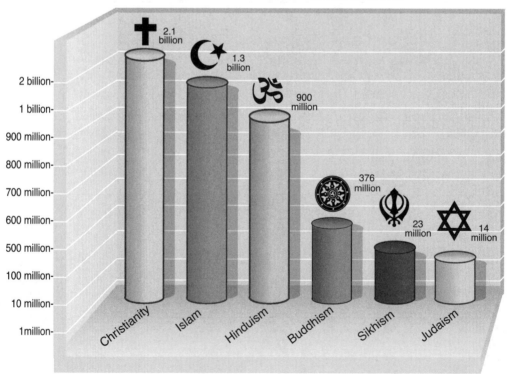

Christianity	2.1 billion
Islam	1.3 billion
Hinduism	900 million
Buddhism	376 million
Sikhism	23 million
Judaism	14 million

Source: www.adherents.com

In the 150 years after Nanak's death, nine more gurus further refined the faith, adding new traditions while maintaining the teachings of the faith's founder. The leadership of the ten gurus was essential in meeting the challenges Sikhism and its followers faced over its five-hundred-year history. Through ongoing political and social struggles, Sikhs developed unique practices and articles of faith. These traditions define and differentiate Sikhs from the followers of other religions.

While basic Sikh doctrine has elements in common with the major world religions that preceded it (primarily Hinduism, Buddhism, Islam, but also Judaism and Christianity), Sikh practices are distinctive. For example, Sikhs literally wear the articles of their faith, including turbans, uncut hair and beards, small ceremonial daggers, and metal bracelets.

Aside from visible differences that set Sikhs apart, many Sikhs feel alienated by non-Sikhs' lack of understanding of Sikh history and beliefs. As fifteen-year-old Rasna Rihal, a Sikh living in North Carolina, explains, "The thing I don't like is how my friends keep asking me over and over what my religion is because they can't remember what it's called."[2] Misunderstanding of Sikhism causes some adherents more than frustration. After the September 11, 2001, attacks on the World Trade Center and the Pentagon, many Sikh men were viewed with suspicion because they wear turbans and long beards similar to those worn by terrorist leader Osama bin Laden and members of Afghanistan's brutal Taliban regime.

Sikhs and those who understand the faith portray Sikhism as a progressive religion well suited to modern times. Unlike the religious extremists some Sikhs have been associated with, followers of Sikhism promote cooperation between and acceptance of all faiths and equality between men and women. "My religion believes in equality and freedom. That's what I like about being a Sikh," said Manmohan Singh, a member of a New Jersey Sikh congregation.[3] The challenge for modern Sikhs is to promote understanding between Sikhs and adherents of different religions. The founder of Sikhism took on that same challenge more than five hundred years ago.

chapter | one

The Origins of Sikhism

The Sikh religion originated in the ponderings, insights, and teachings of Nanak, its founder and first guru. Nanak's philosophy in turn grew out of his life experiences. Nanak was greatly influenced by his love and respect for the Hindu religion he was born into, his travels to adjoining Islamic countries, his many visits to and conversations with the holy men of his time, and the religious diversity of his birthplace—the Punjab.

The Punjab

Bordering the foothills of the Himalayas, the Punjab region includes parts of modern-day northern India and southern Pakistan. Known as both the land of five legendary rivers and the gateway to India, the Punjab has a history of conquest by Aryan, Persian, Greek, and Muslim invaders. Beginning in the tenth century A.D., Punjabis endured five centuries of intense conflict. Sometimes they fought outsiders, rebelling against conquerors from the north. Sometimes religious wars erupted between adherents of the region's two predominant faiths, Hinduism and Islam. Warring Hindu clans also clashed with Muslims moving south from Persia and Afghanistan seeking their fortunes in India.

During this time conflicts led to the creation and growth of new religious and political movements that moved away from rigid adherence to the two prevailing faiths of the Punjab and focused on personal piety over scholarship. For example, the Islamic Sufi sect of mystics had a broad concept of higher power called the Realm of Truth instead of Allah, and a Hindu sect that practiced a form of devotion called bhakti stressed communion with one god instead of the many gods and goddesses worshipped in traditional Hinduism. Both defended the lower classes and emphasized service to others.

In the mid-1400s the Punjab came under the rule of the Muslim and Afghan nobleman Bahlol Khan Lodhi. Ruling from the central city of Lahore, Bahlol Khan Lodhi stabilized the region politically and ushered in a period of religious calm. Bahlol Khan Lodhi's tolerance for practitioners of different faiths drew many outsiders to the region; they brought with them eclectic traditions and beliefs, physically, culturally, and spiritually enriching this already fertile land. It was in this atmosphere of

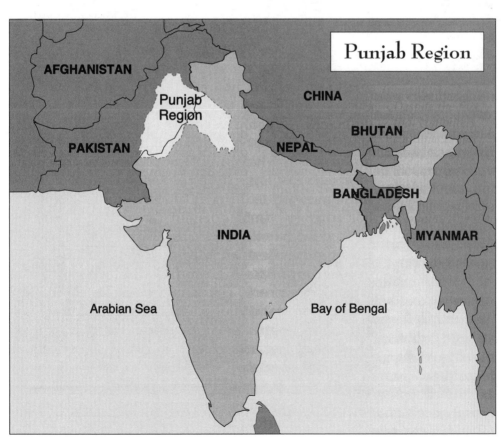

Hindus worship a multitude of gods and goddesses, including the goddess Parvati, portrayed by this statue.

diversity that Guru Nanak Dev Ji, the founder of Sikhism, was born.

A Spiritual Childhood

On April 5, 1469, a Muslim midwife attended the birth of a son to a Hindu couple, Mata Tripta and her husband, Kalyan Chand, a businessman who kept financial records for a wealthy Muslim landowner in the western Punjab village of Talwandi (now part of Pakistan). A Hindu priest and family friends gathered to celebrate the arrival of Kalyan Chand's son, named Nanak, into the world. Both the Hindu priest and Muslim midwife proclaimed the infant an exceptional being with an extraordinary future. The Hindu priest prepared a horoscope that predicted Nanak would become a great philosopher-teacher for both Hindus and Muslims. Early signs that Nanak was a gifted child confirmed his horoscope's prediction, but many believe his philosophy grew as much out of the influences of his birthplace and family as from his questioning mind and superior intellect.

Most accounts of Nanak's childhood suggest he grew up in a traditional middle-class home in a family that accepted and practiced the tenets and doctrines of Hinduism. Those observances included the worship of many gods and goddesses and a belief in a social and religious caste system. The caste system divides Hindu society into four groups, or classes, determined by ancestry and ranked accordingly. The higher the caste a person is born into, the greater his or her social status and opportunities. The highest-ranking caste is reserved for the Brahmans, or Hindu priests; the second-highest, the warriors and rulers; the third, skilled workers and traders; and the fourth, unskilled workers and laborers. Below that caste, literally "outcast," are the so-called untouchables, various groups considered so lowly that for centuries they were relegated to performing the most menial and unpleasant tasks in Hindu society, such as burying the corpses of animals and cleaning sewage from the streets. Nanak was born into the third caste, skilled workers, who generally enjoyed the respect of their community and lived comfortably.

Even as a very young child Nanak possessed an unusual interest in spiritual matters. He began his religious training at school when he was seven years old. Nanak embraced many Hindu beliefs, such as reincarnation—the belief that people are reborn into many different lifetimes for the purpose of spiritual growth. But he also questioned many Hindu religious traditions so expertly that often his teachers could not adequately resolve the philosophical issues he raised. Most of his teachers were so impressed by Nanak's intellect and spiritual insights that they felt they had little to teach him. As one of his teachers explained: "He is a blessed one. He grasps instantly what he hears once."[4]

Nanak quickly mastered mathematics as well as reading and writing in his native Hindi. Later he studied Islamic literature and acquired proficiency in the Persian and Arabic languages. Always inquisitive about the meaning of life, Nanak continued to question his religion throughout his childhood and adolescence, notably at age eleven during an important Hindu rite of passage.

The Sacred Thread Ceremony

The sacred thread ceremony reinforces the Hindu belief in reincarnation. During the ceremony the sons of respected Hindu families must repeat prayers after a Brahman offers and then loops a special knotted thread around each boy from the left shoulder to the right hip. The thread symbolizes a boy's formal entrance into his new life, and he wears it for the rest of that life.

Nanak believed in reincarnation throughout his lifetime, but during his sacred thread ceremony, in front of his family and friends, he refused to accept the sacred thread offered him by the priest. Author Patwant Singh explains how the young Nanak questioned the purpose of wearing the thread: "'Shouldn't deeds, merits and actions,' he asked, 'differentiate one man from another?'"[5] After rejecting the sacred thread, Nanak did something even more baffling; instead of repeating the priest's prayer, he recited his own:

> Make compassion the cotton, contentment the thread,
> Modesty the knot and truth the twist.
> This is the sacred thread of the soul; if you have it, then go ahead and put it on me.
> It does not break, it cannot be soiled by filth; it cannot be burnt or lost.[6]

Nanak meant that the thread itself meant nothing if the person wearing it did not act kindly and honestly toward others.

His sacred thread ceremony would not be the last time Nanak questioned the tenets of Hinduism. Throughout his adolescence Nanak sought the company of many spiritual leaders who visited the Punjab. Those meetings provided the basis of Nanak's developing philosophy.

Seeds of a New Faith

Recognizing his son's remarkable intellect, Kalyan Chand hoped Nanak would follow him into business. The teenage Nanak, however, was content to herd his family's cattle. He spent his time in the fields in meditation and discussion with Hindu and Muslim holy men staying in the forests surrounding his village or traveling through the Punjab. More

than likely, Nanak was exposed to Sufi mystics and bhakti adherents and questioned many of their beliefs and practices. According to Sikh scriptures, he told Hindu holy men that traveling on pilgrimages was not as important as praising the Creator:

Pilgrimages, austere discipline,
compassion and charity.
These, by themselves, bring
only an iota of merit.
Listening and believing with
love and humility in your mind,

Although the Sikh guru Nanak believed in reincarnation, he rejected the Hindu ritual (seen here) of tying a thread around young boys as a symbol of that belief.

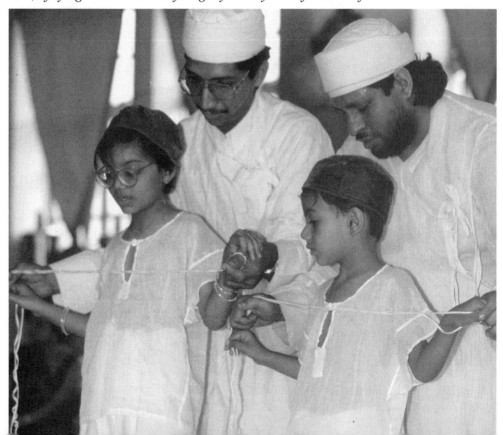

Cleanse yourself with the Name,
At the sacred shrine deep
within.[7]

Similarly, he challenged the purpose of Muslim practices while suggesting more practical ways of living in accordance with the essentials of Islam:

Let mercy be your mosque,
Faith your prayer mat, and
Honest living your Koran.
Make modesty your
circumcision,
And good conduct your fast.
In this way you shall be a true
Muslim.[8]

The diversity of spiritual beliefs in the Punjab and the reflection they inspired influenced Nanak's developing ideas even more than did his early religious education. His exposure to Islamic doctrine, for example, contributed to Nanak's rejection of the caste system and the development of his belief in one all-powerful deity instead of the many gods and goddesses Hindus worshipped. Eventually Nanak decided to devote his life to that god, whom he often referred to as the Divine Creator. For the next several years, however, he was occupied with practical matters.

Sikhism: Founded in an Era of Worldwide Religious Reform

Sikhism can be seen as originating in an era of worldwide religious reform. In the sixteenth century, while Guru Nanak created a new faith incorporating what he believed were the best tenets of Hinduism and Islam, religious reformers in Europe were also leading reform movements to purge Christianity of immorality and unethical practices. Martin Luther, angered by what he saw as corruption in the Roman Catholic clergy, protested against it. The Lutheran denomination of Christianity sprang from Luther's teachings. In France, John Calvin, inspired by Luther's movement, also spoke out against corruption. Calvin is known for promoting Christian Protestantism and founding the Presbyterian Church. Like Nanak, Luther and Calvin spoke out against worshipping idols and emphasized prayer and devotion to God.

Leaving Home and Settling Down

At sixteen Nanak left home to visit his sister Nanaki and her husband, who lived about one hundred miles away in Sultanpur, a city known as a cultural center in the Punjab. Nanak decided to remain in Sultanpur after his brother-in-law recommended him for a job working for Daulat Khan, the governor of the region. Nanak distributed provisions to the people of Sultanpur, kept records, and collected taxes for the governor. He was known to be generous in giving money or food to the poor, often giving more than was required, and some accounts of his life report that somehow supplies never ran out under his watch.

Although Nanak did not particularly like this kind of work, he did appreciate his independence. Within a few years, however, Nanak's sister and father convinced him that his life was incomplete without a wife and children. At the age of nineteen Nanak married a Hindu woman named Sulakhni with whom he had two sons, Sri Chand and Lakhmidas. Although Nanak's family seemed to bring him contentment, he continued to reject Hindu religious rituals. He refused to hold the traditional Hindu ceremony to purify his house

when his first son was born, for instance, declaring birth a natural event and therefore not impure.

While attending to his duties at work and at home, Nanak managed to keep his thoughts on God. Developing a practice that would become a basic Sikh act of faith, Nanak was known to repeatedly recite: "Chanting it, I live; forgetting it, I die."[9] At times his devotion to God seemed to overwhelm him: One Sikh parable relates Nanak's trance-like state, in which he constantly uttered God's name while going about his work dealing out provisions to the people of Sultanpur.

Many who came in contact with Nanak the accountant were impressed by his diligence and attracted by his gracious personality and generous spirit. Some gravitated toward Nanak because of his spirituality. People began congregating at his home for recitations, prayer, and contemplation. Nanak welcomed all visitors. Word of the meetings at his home spread. More people came to hear Nanak talk about his devotion to God, the importance of respecting and accepting different religions, and the equality of all human beings. Eventually Nanak developed a close group of dedicated followers, or disciples, from both the Hindu and Muslim faiths.

For the next several years Nanak seemed happy in his marriage, family life, and his growing circle of friends and disciples. However, while he continued to meditate and pray almost constantly, Nanak was becoming restless spiritually. Then an extraordinary experience changed his life and set him on his religious path.

Bathing at the River Bain

In 1499 Nanak, now thirty years old, went for his usual swim in the River Bain. Leaving his clothing on the shore, Nanak plunged into the waters but did not resurface. For three days and three nights the people of Sultanpur searched for Nanak. Many feared he had drowned. On the fourth day Nanak reappeared on the same spot where he had vanished, went home, and gave away all of his belongings except his loincloth. The people of his village were stunned by Nanak's miraculous return and strange behavior. Crowds gathered to ask Nanak where he had been and what had happened. But Nanak would not speak for a full day after his return.

The next day he broke his silence, saying, "There is no Hindu, no Muslim."[10] Most people misunderstood this message and asked Nanak how he could say Hindus and Muslims do not exist. Nanak meant, however, that though both Hinduism and Islam offer important ideas and attract good people, all faiths are equal in God's eyes.

Nanak then described a mystical encounter with God. At the instant of his disappearance under the water, Nanak explained, he felt he was pulled up into the court of the Creator. Here he was given nectar, a sweet liquid associated with the divine. He drank the nectar and then God spoke to him. In his book *A History of the Sikhs* Khushwant Singh describes Nanak's experience: God called upon Nanak to go out into the world to pray and teach others how to pray. God challenged Nanak to "Let your life be one of praise of the Word, charity, ablution, service and prayer."[11] Nanak answered his Creator in words that would be enshrined in the Sikh scriptures as the Mul Mantra: "True in the Primal Beginning. True Throughout the Ages. True Here and Now. O Nanak, Forever and Ever True."[12]

Nanak came away from this mystical encounter, accepted as the birth of Sikhism, with the certainty that there is only one all-powerful god, the Divine Creator, and that devotion to the Creator is more important than the practice of any individual faith. He thought if people understood what he learned at the River Bain they could accept the basic truths in all

As a guru, Nanak attracted many Sikhs, or disciples. He preached that all faiths are equal in God's eyes.

faiths, overcome their prejudices against others, and serve those less fortunate than themselves. Nanak was also compelled to bring this message of faith to others.

Taking His Message to the People

After Nanak's enlightenment at the River Bain, he became a guru—that is, a spiritual teacher. He set out to spread God's message as he had come to understand it, attracting followers along the way who called themselves Sikhs, a Punjabi word meaning "disciples." Known now as Guru Nanak, he traveled with his friend and fellow Sikh, a Muslim musician named Mardana, to southern India and Ceylon, to Tibet, and to Mecca and Baghdad. Along the way Guru Nanak sang poems of praise as Mardana accompanied him with lilting music. These hymns became the earliest of Sikhism's sacred texts.

Hymn Sung During Travels with Mardana

Guru Nanak and Mardana traveled north of the Punjab into the foothills of the Himalayas. Here they met some yogis (Hindu holy men) who had decided to live like hermits in the forest as a way to reach salvation. Guru Nanak told them they could never attain peace and everlasting joy by discarding worldly life. When asked by the yogis what they should do, Nanak replied with the following hymn, recorded in the Guru Granth Sahib as Ramkali Mohalla 1, 943: 4–6.

> Destroy the feeling of egoism,
> Destroy the sense of duality and attain oneness with [the] Lord,
> The path is hard for [the] ignorant and egoistic;
> But those who take shelter in the Word and are absorbed in it,
> And he who realizes that He is both within and without,
> His fire of desire is destroyed by the Grace of the Guru,
> Says Nanak.

Guru Nanak (center) and the Muslim musician Mardana wrote the hymns that comprise the earliest sacred texts of Sikhism.

He also met many scholars, mystics, and holy men from both Hinduism and Islam. Guru Nanak believed both faiths expressed divine truths. His developing philosophy incorporated his appreciation for the Hindu virtue of compassion and the idea of equality promoted by Islam.

Although he respected many of the teachings of Hinduism and Islam, however, Guru Nanak disapproved of many practices of both religions, believing them to be inconsistent with the faiths' divine truths. For example, he disagreed with the discriminatory treatment of women basic to both faiths and the Hindu caste system. Guru Nanak also criticized what he viewed as meaningless rituals replacing faith and devotion to God. He spoke out against the Hindu practice of worshipping idols representing various Hindu deities. He once told a Hindu priest it was better to give food to the hungry than to make sacrifices to the gods and goddesses of Hinduism.

Guru Nanak's faith in God was so strong that he voiced his criticism without fear of powerful and influential Hindu priests or Muslim leaders. He demonstrated the modesty and humility he encouraged people of both faiths to show in every thought and action: "As he submits to God's Will, and surrenders to the Creator, he is rid of selfishness and conceit,"[13] he wrote.

Preaching Against Discrimination

On their journeys Guru Nanak and Mardana witnessed and spoke out against inequality among people. In many areas they found poor people struggling to obtain life's basic necessities while the wealthy lived idle lives, their needs and wants filled by servants. While in southern India Guru Nanak condemned the caste system that discriminated against the poorest of Hindu society. Wherever he observed discrimination or Hindu/Muslim animosity and ongoing conflict over religious control of a particular area, he preached about the need for tolerance and respect for all faiths.

Guru Nanak was particularly moved by the plight of women. For the most part, Hindu and Muslim women were little more than the property of their husbands. Few women were allowed to participate in religious services. Guru Nanak accepted men and women followers and insisted that both be treated equally. One of his poems, recorded in sacred Sikh texts, stresses the importance of women to all life:

From woman, man is born;
within woman, man is
conceived;
To woman he is engaged and
married. Woman becomes his
friend, through woman the
future generations come.
When his woman dies, he
seeks another woman;
To woman he is bound.
So why call her bad? From
her, kings are born.
From woman, woman is
born; without woman, there
would be no one at all.[14]

Choosing the Carpenter's Food

Guru Nanak's fame grew with each journey from his native Punjab. In time each return to the area of his birth was hailed as the return of a great holy man. But Guru Nanak rejected the recognition of the wealthy Punjabi rulers, preferring to spend his time with common laborers and small farmers. Parables of his life underscore his commitment to humility and hard work.

For example, it is said that in the western Punjab village of Saidpur, Guru Nanak stayed in the home of a carpenter named Lalo. Upon hearing of the guru's visit, a descen-dent of a well-known Brahman and prominent Hindu official of the area invited him to a banquet he was hosting to honor holy men. At first, Guru Nanak refused to attend, saying he preferred the company of the poor. Later he decided to attend the event but declined to eat. When asked why, he told the official his food tasted rancid next to that of the carpenter's because "Lalo earns with the sweat of his brow and out of it offers whatever little he can to the wayfarer, the poor and the holy, and so it tastes sweet and wholesome, but you being without work, squeeze blood out of the people through bribery, tyranny and show of authority."[15] In one version of this story, Guru Nanak performed a miracle by actually squeezing blood from the Hindu official's food.

Guru Nanak also believed in showing devotion to God through prayer and meditation and service to humankind. Earning one's living by honest means and hard work indeed became one of the defining principles of Sikhism. This simple and inclusive spiritual philosophy appealed to a wide range of people, especially the marginalized but also the rich and powerful, and the body of Sikhs following him and his teachings continued to grow.

Sikhs prepare the communal meal, or langar, *for the thousands of daily visitors to the Golden Temple in Amritsar.*

Coming Home to the Punjab

After several years of traveling, Guru Nanak returned to the Punjab and found a quiet spot near the Ravi River just north of the city of Lahore. There he settled with his wife and two sons and farmed the land. By now he was a well-known and influential holy man. People came from far and near to hear his poems and hymns praising God. Followers gathered for morning and afternoon worship led by Guru Nanak. The Sikhs pledged their loyalty and service to Nanak and his teachings and their faith and devotion to God. As Sikhs settled nearby, the guru's home became the center of a village called Kartarpur. In this first Sikh community spiritual education and the beliefs established by Nanak thrived.

Anyone traveling through the Punjab was welcome in Kartarpur. Many visitors chose to stay in the community and adopt the new faith. Some of the converts to the new religion were other Hindu farmers in the Punjab and Hindu merchants from the nearby city of Lahore. A few were Muslims like Nanak's good friend and musical accompanist Mardana.

An important early Sikh practice was offering food and shelter to all, including lower caste Hindus and Muslim peasants. Eventually Guru Nanak established a communal meal service, called a *langar,* as an integral part of Sikh worship. People gathered to prepare and share a meal before worship services. Many poor people found acceptance and hope for salvation through the guru's teachings while many of those seeking divine truth from Nanak found a new faith.

Picking a Successor

For fifteen years Guru Nanak remained the leader of the Sikh community, preaching and otherwise playing a leading role in its activities. In time the question of his successor arose. To Nanak's sons' reported dismay, the guru rejected both of them as his successor because they often refused to do work they considered beneath their dignity.

The story passed down by generations of Sikhs gives the following account of the incident that led to the selection of the second Sikh guru. In 1539 the aged Nanak, his two sons, and his disciple Lehna came across what appeared to be a corpse covered with a piece of cloth. Nanak asked, "Who would eat it?" His sons refused, thinking their father was crazy, but Lehna followed the Guru's suggestion. When he removed the cloth, however, he discovered a tray of sacred food. Lehna first offered the food to the guru and then to Nanak's two sons; he ate only what was left over. The guru then said, "Lehna, you were blessed with the sacred food because you could share it with others. If the people use the wealth bestowed on them by God for themselves alone or for treasuring it, it is like a corpse. But if they decide to share it with others, it becomes sacred food. You have known the secret. You are my image."[16] Guru Nanak then blessed Lehna and gave him the new name of Angad. Nanak then put five coins and a coconut in front of Angad, symbolizing the faith placed in the new guru, and bowed before him. When Nanak gathered his followers together for prayers, he directed Angad to sit in the seat of the guru and called Angad his successor. Nanak's actions set the precedent for Sikh succession: All nine of the gurus following Nanak were installed in the same fashion as Angad.

Guru Nanak often tested his disciples' faith, and time after time Guru Angad proved his worthiness. He had given up his devotion to the Hindu god Durga to follow Nanak after hearing him speak. From the moment of his conversion, Angad had embraced Sikhism's teachings and done whatever was necessary to serve the guru and the Kartarpur community. During the day Angad worked hard on Nanak's farm and spent his free time in prayer and meditation. A few days after Angad passed his final test of faith by uncovering the tray of sacred food, on September 7, 1539, the old guru, Nanak, died peacefully at home.

Guru Nanak's influence was political as well as religious. In his 1849 book *A History of the Sikh People: From the Origins of the Nation to the Battles of the Sutlej* Joseph Davey Cunningham wrote that Guru Nanak laid down broad foundations for social reform of his country which gave "practical effect to the doctrine that the lowest is equal with the highest, in race as in creed, in political rights as in religious hopes."[17] Those leaders of the Sikh religion who followed Nanak retained that focus on social reform despite many spiritual and political challenges.

chapter | two

The Gurus and Development of Sikh Beliefs

As the founder and first guru of Sikhism, Nanak did not claim to be a divine leader, only a spiritually aware teacher who helped his followers better understand God and his creation. The nine Sikh gurus who succeeded Nanak shared his basic philosophy and likewise are recognized as mortal men, enlightened but not divine. According to Sikh scripture each of the ten gurus transferred his spiritual understanding to his successor much like one candle transfers its flame to another candle. Over the next 150 years the gurus would serve a growing number of Sikhs and the new religion by refining, defending, and adding to its essential teachings.

The first five gurus established the faith by writing and collecting sacred Sikh scripture and creating new religious ceremonies, including rituals for marriage, child naming, and funerals. They also organized and built new Sikh centers of worship. Their deeds and words have been passed down as parables and lessons through the centuries, at first orally and then as scriptural texts. These stories of the gurus' humility, kind acts, and devotion to God inspired early Sikhs to help establish Sikh communities throughout the Punjab and beyond its borders.

The third Sikh guru, Guru Amar Das, known for his selfless service to others, is pictured carrying water for Guru Angad's bath.

The Ten Sikh Gurus

Guru Nanak (1469–1539), founder of Sikhism.

Guru Angad (1504–1552) developed Gurmukhi script, a written form of the Punjabi language.

Guru Amar Das (1479–1574) trained Sikh apostles, or masands; institutionalized the communal kitchens, or *langar*.

Guru Ram Das (1534–1581) founded Amritsar.

Guru Arjan Dev (1563–1606) compiled the Granth Sahib and became the first martyr of Sikhism.

Guru Hargobind (1595–1644) instituted weapons training.

Guru Har Rai (1630–1661) reigned during a time of peace.

Guru Harkrishan (1656–1664), known as the boy guru, became guru at age five and died of smallpox at eight.

Guru Tegh Bahadur (1621–1675), second guru martyr for the faith.

Guru Gobind Singh (1666–1708) created the Khalsa, survived the martyrdom of his four sons.

Sikhs revere the ten gurus, some of whom are pictured here, as enlightened human beings and not gods.

The last five Sikh gurus significantly changed the faith to deal with the tumultuous politics of late-seventeenth-century India. During this period the Mogul emperors of India became increasingly antagonistic to all religious sects other than followers of Islam. Under the leadership of later gurus, Sikhs became defenders of their own and other faiths.

Sikh Scriptures

Beginning with Nanak and his musician-companion Mardana, the ten gurus spread their message by reciting and singing poems, hymns, and prayers praising God and his greatness. Through the 1500s and 1600s the gurus wrote down these devotional verses, which were compiled into an evolving work known as the Adi Granth. This work provided the basis and beginning of the holy book of Sikhism. Unlike the scriptures of other world religions that were written by disciples or other writers sometimes centuries after the faith began, the Adi Granth was written by the founders themselves, who describe the book as the direct word of God, revealed through the gurus.

In the sixteenth century the sacred writings of India's other religions were written in Sanskrit or Arabic, both scholarly languages little understood by the masses. The Adi Granth, in contrast, was originally written in a form of Punjabi, the common language, called Gurmukhi. This script was invented by the second guru, Angad, to make Sikh teachings as accessible as possible. His successors followed suit. When one Hindu Brahman asked the third Sikh guru, Amar Das, why he did not instruct his disciples or write his texts in the sacred language of Sanskrit, the guru answered: "Sanskrit is like a well, deep, inaccessible and confined to the elite, but the language of the people is like rain water—ever fresh, abundant and accessible to all." The guru went on to say, "I want my doctrines to be propagated through every language which the people speak, for it is not language but the content that should be considered sacred or otherwise."[18] Like his predecessors Amar Das continued compiling and writing sacred Sikh verses. He also included works by Hindu and Muslim holy men, which gave the Adi Granth the reputation as the essence of many religions.

In 1604 the fifth guru, Arjan Dev, set out to recompile the poems and hymns of the previous gurus, his own writings, and several works of Hindu and Muslim scholars and saints. This work, called the Granth Sahib, is recognized as the essential creed and teachings of Sikhism. It is 1,430 pages long and contains 5,894 sayings and hymns, 974 contributed by the first guru, Nanak.

The first section of the Granth Sahib is particularly important. Known as the Japji, this section of thirty-five short poems by Nanak appeared at the very beginning of the Adi Granth. In lyrical verse these hymns describe the path to salvation, and the core beliefs of Sikhism, in terms of three concepts: the name of God, or Naam; the word of God, or Shabad; and the company of the devout and the virtuous, or Sat Sang.

The first words of the Japji are the short verse called the Mul Mantra, the invocation that names and praises the Divine Creator as the one true God.

The holy book's last poem, written by Guru Arjan Dev, poetically describes the Sikh's three goals:

> Upon this Plate, three things
> have been placed:
> Truth, Contentment, and
> Contemplation.
> The Ambrosial Nectar of the
> Naam, the Name of our Lord
> and Master,
> Has been placed on it as well; it
> is the Support of all.
> One who eats it and enjoys it
> shall be saved. [19]

Achieving these goals depends first on constant consciousness of God.

Devotion to One God

Sikhs believe in and worship one god, the Divine Creator. As the Mul Mantra states, this deity is the creator of Earth and everything on Earth but far greater than his creation. The Divine Creator is omnipotent (all-powerful), omniscient (all-knowing), and omnipresent (exists in all things). The god Sikhs worship is also formless, which means he cannot be born into human form in the way Christians believe Jesus Christ existed on earth. Sikhs believe God cannot be comprehended by a human's five senses and can only be perceived through prayer, meditation, and devotion. This includes the concept of constant repetition of God's name as a doorway to salvation.

Sikhs define devotion not as worshipping God through idols or sacrifice but as living a good and decent life, cultivating humility, helping others, and striving to keep God first in their minds at all times. The second guru, Angad, demonstrated his humble devotion to God first by going into seclusion after Nanak's death. Humbled by his position as leader of the Sikhs and saddened by the death of his mentor, Angad prayed and meditated for six months before taking his place as guru. Many Sikhs view this act as a testing of the strength of Guru Angad's faith.

Guru Amar Das and the Turbans

When the third guru, Amar Das, served his predecessor by supervising the construction of the Sikh settlement Goindwal on the River Beas, he would get up early in the morning and carry water from the river to the guru. Each year Guru Angad gave Amar Das a turban in honor of his devotion. Indeed, Amar Das was so devoted that over the years he wore the turbans one on top of the other, refusing to ever throw away any gift from his guru. People often ridiculed Amar Das for such blind faith but he just ignored them, and today the turban is an important article of faith in Sikhism.

A Sikh man wears a large, elaborate turban. Turbans are an article of faith that is central to Sikhism.

Many Sikh stories promote humility and service as the highest means of winning others' support. One example is the story of Guru Nanak's son Sri Chand, who in his old age journeyed with the fourth guru, Ram Das. At journey's end Sri Chand asked Guru Ram Das why he chose to wear his beard so long. Ram Das fell to his knees and exclaimed, "To wipe the dust off the feet of holy men like yourself." [20] Ram Das proceeded to wipe Sri Chand's feet clean with his beard. Sri Chand was so moved by Ram Das's act that he pledged his devotion and service to the fourth guru.

Spiritual Evolution

Sikhs adopted the Hindu concept of reincarnation—the idea that a soul is born into a sequence of many different lives on Earth in a process of spiritual evolution. Eventually, when the individual soul has achieved enlightenment and no longer needs or seeks earthly desires, it can escape the cycle of physical birth and rebirth and join with the divine for eternity.

Sikhs also believe in karma, the law of cause and effect that determines a soul's evolution. The good or bad done in a previous life affects a soul's present life, and one's actions in this life affect subsequent lives. According to a Sikh Web site, Guru Nanak explained that present acts cannot undo past wrongs:

"The recorded deeds cannot be effaced because God has recorded them." [21] However, like Hindus, Sikhs believe people can change the course of their destinies by the way they live their lives. Though birth is determined by karma, a soul's ultimate liberation comes through complete submission to and devotion to God's word, by virtuous living and deeds, and by God's grace. Superficial practices or simply reciting or chanting of religious mantras is insufficient.

Sikhs believe spiritual evolution is achieved in five stages. In the first stage, called Dharam Khand, a spiritually unaware person performs his or her duty sincerely. In the second stage, Gian Khand, the devotee becomes aware of the greatness of God and God's attributes. A Sikh achieves purity of mind and understanding in the third stage, Saram Khand. In the fourth stage, Karam Khand, by his good works a devotee acquires divine grace; and in the fifth and final stage, Such Khand, through divine grace the devotee enters the Divine Creator's realm, which is beyond reality and human existence, and dwells there for eternity.

Sikhs reject several Hindu practices related to the concepts of reincarnation and karma, preferring to see spiritual progress as an individual's unique journey. Primarily, Sikhs believe social caste—such as the Hindu caste system, by which large groups of people are classified—is irrelevant to spiritual growth. Honest work that contributes to the community is important regardless of one's circumstances. The third guru, Amar Das, explained that Sikhs should "Do good to others by giving good advice, by setting a good example, and by always having the welfare of mankind in your heart."[22]

Sikhs believe in self-reliance and service to those in need. Guru Amar Das devoted much of his time to helping the sick and the elderly, and he insisted all Sikh communities provide for the needy. Under Amar Das's leadership all Sikh worship centers, called *gurdwaras*, featured *langars*, the traditional community kitchens, and all visitors were fed before attending worship services. The story is told of the Muslim emperor Akbar, who stopped in a Sikh community on his way to Lahore. Expecting to see Guru Amar Das, the emperor was told to eat in the *langar* first. There he found himself in the company of the poorest of the poor. Impressed by a community open to people from all walks of life, Akbar offered to help support the *langar* with a gift of the revenues collected from several villages. Amar Das refused the offer, saying the *lan-*

gar must be self-supporting and dependent only upon the offerings of the devout.

Acceptance of All Faiths

Visitors to *gurdwaras* were not restricted to Sikhs. Sikhs believe, as all gurus preached, that all faiths are equal in God's eyes. The second guru, Angad, is quoted in the Granth Sahib as saying, "How can anyone be called bad? We have only One Lord and Master. . . . He watches over us all."[23] The gurus demonstrated their acceptance of other faiths in several ways. They encouraged those from other faiths to worship with them. Sikhs and non-Sikhs all sat on the floor at the same level to share a meal in the *langar.*

The gurus also showed respect for the philosophies and writings of other faiths. For example, the fifth guru, Arjan Dev, declared all religions the same by saying all worship the same God, only under different names: "Some call it Rama; Some call it Khuda; Some worship it as Vishnu; some as Allah."[24] Several decades later the tenth guru, Gobind Singh, went even further, saying all forms of worship are the same, "Hindus and Muslims are one! The same Reality is the creator and preserver of all; Knows no distinctions between them. The monastery and the mosque are the same. So are the Hindu form of

A Sikh woman carries the Granth Sahib, the Sikh holy book, into the temple.

worship and the Muslim prayer. Humans are all one!"[25]

Despite the gurus' tolerant attitude toward other faiths, Sikhs rejected rituals they considered meaningless and practices they believed to be discriminatory. Fourth guru Ram Das explained, "Birth and caste are of no avail before God. It is deeds which make or unmake a man." Ram Das went on to say,

> To wash one's sins not through compassion and self-surrender, but through ablutions; to insist upon special diets, languages and dresses, and fads about what to eat and what not, and to condemn the mass of human beings, including women, to the status of sub-humans and to deny them the reading of the scriptures and even work of every kind is to tear apart man from man. This is not religion, nor is it religion to deny the world through which alone man can find his spiritual possibilities.[26]

Equality of All Men and Women

While Nanak preached acceptance of all religions, he also taught that all men and women are equal whatever their status at birth or in life. The third guru, Amar Das, reinforced Nanak's philosophy of equality by condemning Hindu and Islamic traditions that discriminated against women and the poor. He spoke against the Hindu caste system, saying, "The entire universe is made of the same clay. The Potter has shaped it into all sorts of vessels."[27]

Amar Das also condemned suttee, a Hindu practice which required new widows to throw themselves upon the funeral pyres of their husbands. He also tried to liberate women from wearing burkas or veils over their faces and preached his approval of widows remarrying. Perhaps Amar Das's most important act against discrimination was to train fifty-two women to be apostles for the Sikh faith. During his leadership (1552–1574) the number of converts to Sikhism grew rapidly—partially due to Amar Das's teaching skills.

Teaching the Faith

While Sikhs today do not believe it is important to make pilgrimages or to actively convert followers, their gurus traveled across India preaching their faith and attracting congregants. Despite his advanced age, third guru Amar Das went on many pilgrimages to spread Sikh doctrine, conducting religious services at sacred

Hindu sites along the banks of the Yamuna and Ganges rivers in India. His simple, direct message emphasized the Sikh principles of equality and service, and Sikhism rapidly gained converts.

Guru Amar Das encouraged and dealt with the rapid growth of the Sikh faith by organizing the Sikh centers throughout India into twenty-two dioceses called *manjis*. The Sikh *manjis* both spread Sikh teachings and collected revenues to sustain the fledgling faith. Amar Das also trained 146 apostles called *masands*, both men and women, who traveled to many parts of the country to preach Sikhism.

Building Amritsar

Important Sikh centers were founded in Lahore and Goindwal in modern-day Pakistan and northern India. Then in 1577 the fourth guru, Ram Das, founded Amritsar, a splendid city that would eventually become the holiest city and spiritual center of Sikhism. In the middle of Amritsar, Ram Das dug a sacred pool in whose waters people bathed for spiritual renewal. The name Amritsar derived from the Sanskrit words *amrit*, meaning elixir of life or sacred water of the divine, and *sarowar*, meaning lake or pool. It was not long before Amritsar became the home of many spiritual leaders and mystics who came to expe-

rience its holy waters; writers, artists, musicians, and scholars who made the city a cultural haven; and the traders and craftsmen who built the city, then settled there permanently.

Arjan Dev, Ram Das's youngest son and fifth guru of the Sikh faith, continued his father's work at Amritsar by building a magnificent temple there. Under Arjan Dev's leadership the foundation for the Sri Harmandir Sahib, which would become known as the Golden Temple, was laid in the middle of the largest sacred pool. At the time, most Sikhs wanted the temple to be the tallest building in the growing city, but the fifth guru had it constructed at as low an elevation as possible to remind Sikhs of the importance of humility. In keeping with the Sikh belief in self-reliance and to raise money for the temple's construction, the guru declared all Sikhs should donate one-tenth of their earnings to charity, another practice that became a central tenet of Sikhism.

The temple at Amritsar blended Hindu and Muslim architectural styles, with one distinct feature. Muslims believe that God's house is entered from the west and Hindus believe that it is entered from the east. In contrast to those faiths, the Harmandir has doors on all four sides. "My faith is for the people of all castes and all creeds from

The Golden Temple stands at the center of the largest sacred pool in Amritsar, the spiritual center of Sikhism.

whichever direction they come and to whichever direction they bow,"[28] said Guru Arjan Dev. The sixth guru, Hargobind, continued expanding Amritsar by building another temple facing the Harmandir. From this spiritual house, called Akal Takht, Hargobind administered the affairs of the Sikh faith, which began to be threatened in the early 1600s.

The Dasam Granth—Another Sacred Text of Sikhism

The Dasam Granth, a collection of verse primarily written by the tenth guru Gobind Singh, is another sacred text of Sikhism. The 1,400-page work was compiled by Sikh scholar Bhai Mani Singh and first published in 1734. Some sections of the

Dasam Granth are autobiographical, describing the tenth guru's childhood in the Himalayas and his battles with Mogul emperors. Others are religious meditations, the best known being the Jaap, which praises the characteristics and power of God. Instead of describing what God is, Gobind Singh often wrote about what God is not as in this excerpt from the Jaap: "God has no marks or symbols, no colour or caste, not even family lineage. God's form, hue, shape, and dress can be described by no one. God is immovable and self-existent. God shines in no borrowed splendour. No one can measure God's might."

The tenth and last guru, Gobind Singh, simplified and reformed the Sikh faith.

Martyrs and Militarism

Since Nanak's time Mogul emperors had allowed Sikhism to grow and thrive. That situation changed with the death of Emperor Akbar in 1605. Akbar's successor Jahangir was not supportive of the Sikhs or any other religion besides Islam. In his memoirs Jahan-gir wrote about the fifth Sikh guru, Arjan Dev, and his followers, "Many innocent Hindus and even foolish and ignorant Muslims he brought into his fold who beat the drum noisily of his self-appointed prophethood. For a long time I had harbored the wish that I should set aside this shop of falsehood or I should bring him into the fold of Islam."[29]

When Arjan Dev refused to renounce his beliefs and convert to Islam, he was tortured to the point of death. On May 30, 1606, Arjan Dev bid his followers goodbye and let his broken body be carried away by the waters of the Ravi River. Arjan Dev thus became the first martyr of Sikhism.

The death of Arjan Dev changed the direction of the Sikh faith. Arjan Dev's son and successor, Hargobind, though only eleven years old, understood Sikhism was threatened. At his installation as the sixth guru he placed two swords on either side of him—one symbolizing spirituality and the other, power. Hargobind asked Sikhs to make offerings of horses and weapons rather than money, and he encouraged physical activity and weapons training as well as quiet meditation.

Within a decade the Sikhs had prepared themselves to defend their faith and bring justice to the Punjab by military force if necessary. In 1617, upon hearing of Hargobind's arming of the Sikhs, Emperor Jahan-gir called the sixth guru to Delhi and kept him a virtual prisoner there for several months, held with other political prisoners in deplorable conditions. An admirer of the guru eventually convinced the emperor to release Hargobind, but the guru refused to leave until the emperor agreed to free all the other prisoners.

Over the next few decades the Sikhs' relationship with India's emperors continued to deteriorate as intermittent violent clashes broke out between the Muslim armies and the Sikhs. By the time of the ninth guru, Tegh Bahadur, India's rulers were attempting to eliminate all religions but Islam. In 1675 the emperor 'Alamgir ordered India's provincial governors to immediately destroy Sikh schools and temples and outlaw Sikh teachings and practices. 'Alamgir also ordered the execution of all who refused to embrace Islam. Sikhs and Hindus alike sought Guru Tegh Bahadur's help. Tegh Bahadur offered himself to the emperor, declaring that if 'Alamgir could force him to convert to Islam, the Sikhs and Hindus would also abandon their faiths.

The emperor arrested the guru, put him in an iron cage, and forced him to witness the execution of three of his closest friends and followers: According to Sikh history, one was sawn in two, the second was boiled to death, and the third was burned alive. Still the guru would not renounce his faith. Finally Guru Tegh Bahadur was publicly beheaded, becoming the second Sikh guru to die for his beliefs.

The Sikh gurus' martyrdom cemented their followers' resolve to defend their religion and the rights of all people to worship God as they choose, winning the support of oppressed peoples including many Hindus and poor, struggling Muslims. A new, militant faction of Sikhism evolved, establishing a tradition that has influenced non-Sikhs' perception of the faith to the present day.

The Creation of the Khalsa

Gobind Singh was only nine years old when the severed head of his father, Guru Tegh Bahadur, was delivered to his family for cremation. Succeeding his father as the tenth and last guru, Gobind Singh recognized his mission early in life. In his autobiography, he wrote that God charged him with the duty of upholding moral law, preserving equality among people, and destroying sin and evil: "I took birth to see that righteousness may flourish: that the good may live and tyrants be torn out by their roots."[30] In taking up this cause Gobind Singh created both a means of recruiting courageous and righteous defenders of Sikhism and the practice of Sikh baptism.

Gobind Singh believed the lessons of Nanak and the other gurus—that love and forgiveness are stronger than hate and revenge. However, as he wrote in his autobiography, his life experience taught him to resist enemies of the faith, violently if necessary: "When all other means have failed it is permissible to draw the sword."[31]

In 1699 Gobind Singh sent out messengers inviting all Sikhs to come to his headquarters at Anandpur with their hair and beards uncut. After a worship service, the guru asked for five volunteers to be sacrificed for the faith. The congregation grew fearful but finally one man stepped forward to give up his life. Gobind Singh took the man into a tent and returned

The fifth Sikh guru, Guru Arjan Dev, was tortured to death for refusing to convert to Islam. He became the first Sikh martyr.

shortly thereafter holding a bloody sword. He asked for another volunteer and another followed him into the tent. Eventually three more men agreed to be sacrificed.

After the last of the five had entered the tent, the guru reemerged, followed by the five volunteers, all dressed in turbans and saffron-colored robes. The blood on Guru Gobind Singh's sword was that of a slaughtered goat. Gobind Singh declared that the five who were willing to die for their faith would henceforth be known as the beloved ones, the first members of a new Sikh community.

Each of the five was then baptized in a new way. The guru mixed sugar in water, stirring it with a clean sword. He then asked the men to drink the mixture while hymns were recited. Then Gobind Singh turned

A Sikh baptizes a devotee with amrit, a solution of consecrated sugar-water.

to the men and asked them to baptize him in the same manner. Gobind Singh declared he was no longer their superior but their brother and called them members of the Khalsa, or pure ones. They were to renounce their old occupations and become soldiers, sever family ties to become part of the Gobind family, reject earlier creeds for that of the Khalsa, and give up all rituals except those of the Sikh faith.

Gobind Singh united the Sikhs with the creation of the Khalsa. The beloved ones, originally from different walks of life, were all given a new surname, Singh, which means lion. Today men and women choosing to be baptized as Sikhs are initiated into the faith in a ceremony much like the baptism of Guru Gobind Singh and the five beloved ones. Through baptism they are reborn as new men and women, without caste or religious differences.

Members of the Khalsa were ordered never to cut their hair, smoke or chew tobacco, or drink alcohol. They were prohibited from eating an animal killed by being bled to death (also a rule of Islam) and from harassing or harming Muslim women despite the fact that they were virtually at war with Muslim authorities. Within just a few days after this first initiation ceremony, fifty thousand more Sikhs joined the Khalsa. Guru Gobind Singh declared, "The Khalsa shall rule. Their enemies will be scattered. Only they that seek refuge will be saved." [32] In the battles that followed, Gobind Singh lost his own four sons, but the Khalsa prevailed against overwhelmingly larger armies, victorious by the grace of God, according to Sikh teachings.

Sikhism Is Reformed

The tenth Sikh guru simplified the faith and unified its followers not only by encouraging the most devout to defend Sikhism but also by eliminating corruption in Sikh institutions. For example, he abolished the institution of the *masands,* or apostle teachers. Many *masands* had set up Sikh communities, abused their own power, and extorted money from poor Sikhs. While disbanding the *masands* diminished offerings to the Sikh faith, it helped to protect devotees from unscrupulous officials.

Shortly before his death in 1708, Guru Gobind Singh placed five coins and a coconut, the symbols made sacred by the first guru, Nanak, before the Granth Sahib, declaring the holy book to be the Sikhs' final guru. The term *guru* was now taken to mean both "teacher" and "Word of God," who were one and the same, so the book was to be

Two Sikhs gaze reverently at a copy of the Granth Sahib, or Sikh holy book, which is covered in embroidered cloth under the canopy.

called the Guru Granth Sahib. Wherever it is placed is considered a *gurdwara*, or place to worship God.

Guru Gobind Singh strengthened Sikhism, keeping its doctrine of equality and tolerance but giving congregants a more specific code of ethics and conduct, which differentiated Sikhism from other faiths. By creating the Khalsa he gave the faith an institution for its defense. The Khalsa and its influence would make the Sikhs a powerful political and social force in Indian history.

chapter three

Building an Empire

For the next 350 years Sikhism spread, first throughout northern India and slowly around the world, taking on a more political and militant aspect in response to volatile and changing times. Sikhism managed to survive and sometimes thrive, first, under the rules of intolerant Islamic emperors, then British colonial authorities, and in the twentieth century, the struggling leaders of an independent Indian state.

Revolt Against Muslim Moguls

In the early eighteenth century, Sikhs emerged as defenders of various religious sects facing persecution from India's Islamic rulers. The Mogul emperors who tried to force Sikhs and Hindus to abandon their faiths and convert to Islam found many of their efforts thwarted by the growing number of Khalsa members. Sikh education now included weapons training and combat and attack skills. Sikh military leaders, determined to protect the right to practice their faith, clashed with imperial troops in violent skirmishes throughout the Punjab.

A man who spent much of his early life in Hindu monasteries before his conversion to Sikhism succeeded the tenth guru as leader of the Khalsa upon Guru Gobind Singh's death in 1708. Banda Singh Bahadur made the Khalsa an effective fighting force while leading its members in a decades-long campaign against Mogul troops. Under Banda's leadership, the Khalsa's strategy turned from defense to offense to avenge the death and persecution of Sikhs. In 1709 Banda and his men attacked the town of Samana, where the men who killed Gobind Singh's father and sons lived. The assault on Samana was quick and deadly. According to one account ten thousand men died in the attack.

The poverty of Muslim peasants and the discrimination against all Hindus, especially those in lower castes, created bitter resentment of the Mogul Empire and more recruits for Banda Singh and the Khalsa. Khafi Khan, a Muslim chronicler of the time, wrote that Banda would not impose religious restrictions on anyone, Hindu or Muslim. His fight was specifically directed "against the tyranny of the local Mughal officials

A group of modern-day Sikhs on horseback participates in an annual festival honoring the courageous spirit of Sikh warriors throughout the centuries.

in Punjab, and their high-handedness was resented and opposed not only by the Sikhs and Hindus but also by the Muslims who joined his army in thousands to fight against the Mughal government."[33]

The Sikhs' successes in clash after clash contributed to the weakening of the Mogul Empire in India, and Afghan invaders from the north eventually claimed the Punjab. Meanwhile, Sikh military strength gradually became political power; a century later another Sikh military leader would build and rule an empire in the Punjab.

The Sikh Empire of Ranjit Singh

In the early eighteenth century various invasions and conquerors fractured India into localized kingdoms or chiefdoms. One of those conquering powers was Great Britain. A great naval power since the mid-1500s, the British had developed a colonial empire on several continents. Long a trading partner of India, Great Britain gained control over much of southern India, but northern regions remained in the control of Sikh, Hindu, and Muslim leaders. One Sikh set out to extend his control in the north. His name was Ranjit Singh.

Born on November 13, 1780, Ranjit Singh became the chief and ruler of the Punjab's Sukerchakia region after his father's death in 1790. Both his father and grandfather were known as brave military leaders and shrewd politicians, and Ranjit Singh followed their example. Despite having no formal education, a small, slight stature, and scars from a childhood bout of smallpox—which also left him blind in one eye—Ranjit Singh was a formidable presence.

In July 1799, shortly before his nineteenth birthday, Ranjit Singh and his troops rode into Lahore, capturing it from Afghan rulers and establishing his own headquarters and royal court there. In April 1801 he crowned himself maharaja of the Punjab, although he would not achieve complete control of the entire region until 1809. Under Ranjit Singh's leadership, the number of Sikhs in northern India grew to more than 10 million. Soon the young maharaja was in direct competition with the British for control of India. In a letter dated October 17, 1808, Archibald Seton, a British authority in Delhi, wrote his foreign secretary N.B. Edmonstone, describing Ranjit Singh as "an ambitious, restless and warlike character . . . whose conduct and growing power it is necessary to watch with a jealous and vigilant attention."[34] The British policy became containment of the Sikh empire within its 1809 boundaries.

While wary of the young maharaja's success, many British authorities welcomed the stability it brought to the area. That stability was largely a result of Ranjit Singh's benevolent treatment of conquered peoples. Unlike most rulers of his time, Ranjit Singh did not execute his defeated foes. He allowed them to leave peacefully and often he offered them financial settlements for their losses. He also forbade his soldiers from harassing, molesting, or robbing the citizens of his empire, who comprised not only Sikhs but millions of Hindus and Muslims as well.

In the early nineteenth century Great Britain directed most of its military might against France, whose emperor Napoléon waged wars of conquest in Europe. After Napoléon signed a treaty with Russian czar Alexander I in 1807, the British feared the French general might march his armies through the Punjab into India, taking over British interests there. The British believed Ranjit Singh's strong presence in northern India could ward off any invasion by the French, and so they supported his efforts to consolidate his rule to protect their own landholdings in India. Ranjit Singh used his strategic value to gain more territory and consolidate power.

The Punjab was relatively peaceful and prosperous during Ranjit Singh's thirty-eight-year rule. His power earned him both the respect and concern of other leaders in India, including the British. As English author John Keay wrote, Ranjit Singh's empire was the "most formidable non-colonial state in India,"[35] for more than thirty years.

Ranjit Singh maintained his empire by applying Sikh principles in political matters and treating all of his subjects fairly. As ruler of the Punjab, he once said: "God intended that I look upon all religions with one eye; that is why I was deprived of the other eye."[36] Aware that his new subjects hailed from many faiths, he honored them by supporting Islamic mosques and Hindu temples in his jurisdiction. He appointed both Hindus and Muslims to high positions in his court and his army.

Ranjit Singh also supported his own faith by encouraging the construction of more Sikh *gurdwaras*. Perhaps his most important contribution to Sikhism was the restoration of the great temple at Amritsar, including cladding it in gold leaf. From that point on the holy shrine has been known as the Golden Temple.

The Remarkable Ranjit Singh

Born on November 13, 1780, Ranjit Singh was known as Kaana, or "the one-eyed." He was also short, physically scarred by an early bout of smallpox, and had no formal education. Despite those facts, Ranjit Singh crowned himself the maharaja of Punjab at the age of twenty after conquering and consolidating the northern half of India.

Full of ambition and intense energy, Ranjit Singh was a driven man in his political and his personal life. He was known to have won over subjects by appearing to be a man of the people, preferring to sit on the floor rather than on a throne. Most of all Ranjit Singh loved riding horses. According to writer K.S. Duggal in his book *Ranjit Singh: A Secular Sikh Sovereign,* "The moment he (Ranjit Singh) sat on horseback his ill-looking countenance was completely transformed. Every muscle of his body seemed to vibrate. There was a glow on his face."

While proud of being a Sikh, Ranjit Singh ignored many traditions of his faith in his personal life. He was known to enjoy all-night parties, drinking alcohol, and smoking tobacco. He was also believed to have had more than twenty different wives as well as a sizeable harem.

In 1801 Ranjit Singh crowned himself maharaja of the entire Punjab.

Collapse of the Sikh Empire

Ranjit Singh proved to be an extraordinary leader whose empire could not be maintained without him. After his death on June 27, 1839, his empire soon broke down into the fractured states that existed before he came to power. The British, no longer threatened by French intervention in India after the defeat of Napoléon in 1815, took advantage of the broken alliances, growing corruption, and incompetent leadership of Ranjit Singh's immediate successors to bring all of India under their colonial rule.

Amid Sikh instability, the British employed agents to provoke the Sikhs to break their treaties and go to battle. In December 1845 tensions erupted in the first Anglo-Sikh War. The Sikhs fought valiantly but were eventually outnumbered by British troops. On March 9, 1846, the two sides signed the Treaty of Lahore, which gave the British control over all Sikh holdings between the Sutlej and the Beas rivers, an area covering nearly half of the Punjab. The British then relinquished some territory to Gulab Singh, a Sikh official who had collaborated with the enemy, and appointed him maharaja of Kashmir, a title that did not disguise his alliance with the British.

On November 22, 1848, the second Anglo-Sikh war broke out farther north on the River Chenab. Within months it ended with the defeat of the remaining Sikh empire. As British governor-general Charles Stewart Harbinge wrote to his sister in a letter dated December 14, 1847,

> Who would have ventured to assert that within the short space of 60 days the proud Sikh would have seen the English colors on the walls of Lahore, his forces annihilated, and the descendant of Runjeet Singh thrown on the mercy & forbearance of a British govt. Now "c'est un fait accompli" & with what results? The days of revolutions, murder, & intrigue have passed away, and the Punjab in the memory of man has never known such repose & prosperity.[37]

For the next century, the Punjab was part of British colonial India.

Sikhs Under British Rule

The British dismantled the Sikh empire by disbanding the Sikh army and dividing the Punjab into twenty-seven districts. The new administrative structure was designed to further the development of the Punjab into a prosperous investment for Great Britain. The colonial rulers taxed Punjabis to pay for the construction of new roads, railways, canals, and telegraph offices. These developments, built with native Punjabi labor, increased agricultural production and brought prosperity to British colonial officials operating trading houses, banks, and the shipping industry in the region.

Under British rule, many former Sikh soldiers joined the British colonial army. These Sikh troops were deployed to China to help quell a rebellion in 1901.

The Crown Jewel That Belonged to Ranjit Singh

In the course of conquering different regions to create his Sikh empire, Ranjit Singh also acquired great wealth and some unique and prized possessions. One was the Koh-i-Noor diamond which the wife of an Afghan shah pledged to Ranjit Singh in exchange for sanctuary for her family from marauding Muslims.

The 186-carat jewel—often referred to as the Mountain of Light—had a legendary reputation. Whoever owned the Koh-i-noor, it was said, ruled the world. The gem was so sought after that the British negotiated for it in 1849 as a term of the Treaty of Lahore. Today the Koh-i-Noor diamond is part of the British crown jewels. It is the largest gem in the 1902 coronation crown of Queen Alexandra and is on display at the Tower of London in England.

Today part of the British crown jewels, the Koh-i-Noor diamond was once in the possession of Ranjit Singh.

During this period the British took advantage of the particular talents and skills of the Sikhs, both as farmers and as soldiers. Many former Sikh soldiers joined the British colonial army; their military service was rewarded with grants of land in the Punjab. Eventually Punjabis made up three-fifths of the British Indian army, and the majority of those Punjabis were Sikhs.

Successful Sikhs, like other successful Indians, were expected to blend in with the British colonials. As historian H.R. Mehta wrote, the British worked to create "a class of persons, Indian in blood and colour and British in taste and opinions, in morals and in intellect."[38] In this regard employment of Sikhs in the British Indian army and administrative functions did subject the Sikhs to considerable British influence, but that did not extend to conversion to Christianity.

Missionaries

Beginning in the mid-nineteenth century, European and American Christian missionaries flocked to India to convert Hindus, Muslims, and particularly Sikhs, in the belief that Christianity was a civilizing influence over backward faiths. The British colonial government strongly supported the Christian mission movement and Indian converts. Western missionaries were particularly hopeful when Ranjit Singh's son Dalip converted to Christianity. However, in most cases the missionaries' efforts had the opposite effect. Because many missionaries ignored the fact that for centuries Sikhs had been willing to die for their faith, conversions fell well below expectations. By 1881 only four thousand Sikhs had converted to Christianity.

A religious backlash developed, and a revival of Sikh fundamentalism grew, affecting British interests in India. Hindu and Islamic revivalism also emerged in the Punjab. One Sikh movement led by Ram Singh countered both missionary zeal and colonial rule by avoiding and in some cases boycotting everything British. British authorities, who feared a Sikh rebellion, responded to the movement by keeping Ram Singh and his followers under tight surveillance. Movement members were often arrested and jailed for minor offenses. A few of Ram Singh's followers retaliated by attacking some British businesses and government offices. After being swiftly apprehended, they were executed for their crimes without the benefit of a trial.

Another response to the perceived arrogance of Christian missionaries, who made little effort to understand Sikhism, was the Sikh Singh Sabha movement of the mid-1850s. After an 1855 census taken in parts of the Punjab wrongly classified Sikhs as a sect of Hinduism, Sikh scholars known as Sabhas disseminated writings explaining the essence and spirit of the Sikh scriptures. The first Singh Sabha group formed in Amritsar in 1873; another was established in Lahore in 1879. Within the next twenty years, 117 Singh Sabhas had been founded all across the Punjab. With this resurgence of the Sikh faith came more Sikh literature, schools, book clubs, and educational societies. In 1897 a Khalsa college and ten Sikh schools were established in the Punjab, including an exclusive girls' school in Firozpur.

Sikh Gurdwara Act of 1925

As Sikhs reacted to the missionaries' message by clarifying and reviving their own beliefs, a few Sikh groups protested their loss of control over long-established Sikh worship centers, the *gurdwaras*. Beginning in the middle of the nineteenth century, *mahants*, or caretakers appointed by British authorities, had inherited the *gurdwaras*. Most *mahants* were not Sikhs but Hindus, which deeply offended Sikh congregrants. Further insulting the Sikhs was the fact that an employee of the British deputy commissioner administered the Golden Temple at Amritsar, Sikhism's holiest shrine.

The Sikhs wanted their *gurdwaras* and their Golden Temple back. In the early 1920s a Sikh organization, the Shiromani Gurdwara Parbandhak Committee (SGPC), launched a campaign to regain control of Sikh houses of worship. Many Sikhs marched in protests, resulting in more than forty thousand arrests and four hundred deaths in colonial prisons. Eventually the British negotiated terms of concession; on January 19, 1922, a representative of the British colonial government gave the keys to the Golden Temple to Sardar Kharak Singh, the president of the SGPC. It would be another three years before legislation passed ensuring Sikh control of their *gurdwaras*. The Sikh Gurdwara Act of July 25, 1925, made the Sikhs custodians of their spiritual centers. Indian nationalist leader Mohandas K. "Mahatma" Gandhi sent a telegram to SGPC president Sardar Kharak Singh praising the peaceful protest: "First decisive battle for India's freedom won, congratulations." [39]

This late nineteenth century illustration depicts the members of a Catholic mission in Pondicherry, one of the oldest missions in India.

Sikhs and India's Freedom Movement

In the late 1920s, after a century under British rule, the movement for Indian independence became a significant political force. Gandhi led the movement, based on organized nonviolent protests and boycotts aimed at undermining India's British colonial government. Most Sikhs were drawn to Gandhi's rhetoric and tactics of civil disobedience, which Sikhs had employed successfully from 1922 to 1925.

Sikhs participated in many well-publicized protests. The Reverend C.F. Andres, an Anglican priest and follower of Mahatma Gandhi, witnessed Sikh resolve firsthand during one protest against the British:

There were four Akali Sikhs with black turbans facing a band of about two dozen policemen, including two English officers. They were perfectly still and did not move further forward. Their hands were placed together in prayer. Then, without the slightest provocation on their part, an Englishman lunged it [a brass-bound stick] in such a way that his fist which held the staff struck the Akali Sikh just at the collar bone with great force. The blow sent him [the Akali Sikh] to the ground. He rolled over and slowly got up and at once faced the same punishment again. [40]

A few civilian Sikhs rejected non-violent practices to avenge the deaths of innocent Indians, some-

In 1925 Gandhi congratulated Sardar Kharak Singh for regaining control of Sikh houses of worship.

times achieving the status of Sikh martyrs. In 1931 twenty-four-year-old Bhagat Singh became a martyr after killing a British police officer whom Bhagat Singh believed beat to death Lala Lajpat Rai, a well-respected leader of the freedom movement. Bhagat Singh was arrested, convicted, and executed by British authorities and became a symbol of the Indian independence movement. India's first prime minister Jawaharlal Nehru wrote:

> Bhagat Singh did not become popular because of his act of terrorism, but because he seemed to vindicate, for the moment, the honour of Lala Lajpat Rai, and through him of the nation. He became a symbol and within a few months each town and village of the Punjab, and to a lesser extent in the rest of northern India, resounded with his name. Innumerable songs grew up about him, and the popularity that the man achieved was something amazing.[41]

Sikh Activities During World War II

Support for Indian independence continued to grow during World War II (1939–1945). Some one hundred thousand Sikh soldiers fought in the British military during the conflict, and though many remained loyal to the colonial government, others risked their positions to support a free India. Despite the special accommodations British military commanders made to their Sikh troops—such as allowing Sikhs to swear oaths of loyalty on the Guru Granth Sahib and to wear Sikh symbols into battle—Sikh allegiances were not always secure. Most Sikh soldiers still had strong ties to the Punjab; loyalty to their homeland led to several episodes of Sikh insubordination and even mutiny.

In 1940, for example, the Sikh squadron of Central India Horse in Bombay refused to follow orders to ship out of the country. Squadron members were court-marshaled and their leaders deported to the Andaman Islands. Such high-profile refusals to follow orders concerned many British army officials; some even suggested disbanding all Sikh units.

Even more radically, several Sikhs who served in the British army played a role in creating the twenty-thousand-man Indian National Army, which fought against the British as an auxiliary force on the side of the Japanese, the enemy of Great Britain in Asia and the Pacific. The Japanese recruited many Sikhs among British prisoners of war. In fact, Captain Mohan Singh, a British POW, is cited as a primary organizer of the Indian National Army, one-third of whose troops were Sikhs. At the end of the war many Indian National Army soldiers were tried for treason by British authorities.

British officials began independence negotiations with leaders of the Indian nationalist movement soon after the end of the war. Those negotiations culminated in 1948 when India became a free nation with free elections and a democratic government. India's Sikhs celebrated their nation's new status but faced immediate challenges as their Punjab homeland was split in two.

Dividing the Punjab

Perhaps the most controversial issue in the Indian campaign for independence was satisfying the territorial demands of rival Hindu, Muslim, and Sikh populations. Nehru, a Hindu who became India's first prime minister, and his counterpart in the Muslim community, Mohammad Ali Jinnah, worked to bridge the political gap between India's Muslims and Hindus, but in the end a single, united India was not to be. In 1947 the Indian National Congress and the Muslim League agreed to split up the Punjab—its eastern half remained part of India; its western half joined the newly formed Muslim country of Pakistan.

After the division 40 percent of the Punjab's Sikhs lived on the Pakistani side of the border and 60 percent inhabited the Indian side. Divided, the Sikh community became an even smaller minority in both countries. India's Sikhs lost the city of Lahore, Maharaja Ranjit Singh's capital, along with several historic Sikh shrines including Nanakana Sahib, Guru Nanak's birthplace, to Pakistan. Pakistan's Sikhs lost the holy city of Amritsar to India.

The division was a serious blow to many Sikhs. Some advocated the formation of a separate Sikh state to keep the Punjab intact. But as historian Khushwant Singh writes, "The Sikhs' spokesman worded their demand for a Sikh state—not as something inherently desirable but simply as a point in an argument against Pakistan—[which] robbed the suggestion of any chance of serious consideration."[42]

Most Sikhs did not want a separate homeland—they considered themselves part of India's diverse population. Neither did they want the Punjab divided. Those Sikhs living within Pakistan's borders suffered more than just the loss of a country. Considering the history of Sikh persecution under Mogul emperors, many feared they would be mistreated in a primarily Islamic country. Some suffered discrimination and others fell victim to violent clashes between different cultural and religious groups in the new state of Pakistan. In his book *Mission with Mountbatten* Alan Campbell-Johnson writes of the atrocities he saw in a small town near Rawalpindi soon after partition:

We arrived to find that the havoc in the small town was very great. Picking our way through the rubble, we could see that the devastation was as thorough as any produced by fire-bomb raids in the war. This particular commu-

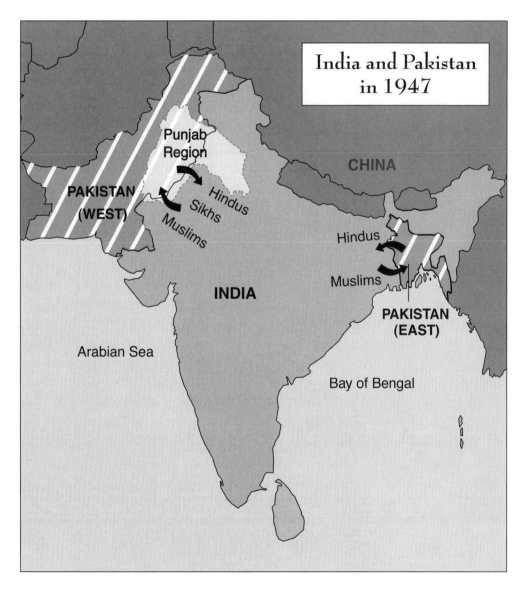

India and Pakistan in 1947

nal orgy involved the destruction of Sikhs and their livelihood by Muslims."[43]

Some Sikhs took revenge upon Muslims living in what was now East Punjab in India. It is estimated that a half million people died in the ethnic and religious violence that followed independence.

Sikh Refugees

In the chaos created by the division of the Punjab, many Sikhs and Hindus on the western side of the border became victims of arson, murder, and looting. It was not long before the division of the Punjab created an exodus of Sikhs and Hindus from Pakistan and an exodus of Muslims from northern India. Leaving the Pakistani side of the Punjab, however, was almost as dangerous as staying. Militant Muslims attacked many refugees attempting to cross the border into India. Thousands died in hostilities on their way to East Punjab.

Emigration meant leaving behind farms, businesses, homes, and friends and neighbors. While Hindu and Sikh refugees struggled to establish

With the partition of India in 1947, millions of Hindu, Muslim, and Sikh refugees crowded onto trains in one of the largest population transfers in history.

themselves in East Punjab, they faced more prejudice from those already living there. Sikh refugees were left with a sense of homelessness and grievance.

In 1948 the leading English-language Punjab newspaper, the *Tribune,* reported the influx of refugees contributed to the already tense relationship between Hindus and Sikhs:

> Let us be honest and admit that it has been there and it has been growing. Its presence and its growth have impeded rehabilitation. Displaced persons are not settling down for fear that they may again be displaced. Communal feeling has not only retarded rehabilitation, it has given it a false accentuation. The two communities that have come across the border are thinking and acting in terms of competitive rather than cooperative rehabilitation. They stand in fear of each other and in fear of the local population. [44]

Hindu extremists gained converts as the Punjab struggled with a growing refugee population, and right-wing political parties that encouraged intolerance and mistrust flourished on all sides.

Some Sikhs looked for new homes outside of India entirely. Waves of emigrants spread the faith to distant places including Australia, England, Burma, Canada, East Africa, and the United States. Many Western countries, including Canada and the United States, had strict immigration laws limiting opportunity for Sikhs and other East Asians, but despite the quota limitations, the immigration of Sikhs from the Punjab to the West in the 1950s was a significant new phase in the spread of the religion. Previously established Sikh communities in England, the United States, and elsewhere were invigorated and strengthened by an influx of new members.

chapter four

The Practices and Traditions of Sikhism

No matter where Sikh communities have taken hold, certain basic practices of the faith are common to all. At the core of Sikh philosophy is the need to seek God, praise God, and keep God in mind at all times. All Sikh religious practices and traditions support that belief by helping congregants reach a state in which their mind is God centered. Sikhs see God not as a being but as a formless, pure force that is both above and present in all human beings. Like Hindus and Buddhists, Sikhs believe a human soul never dies but is reincarnated or reborn into several lifetimes.

Stages of Sikhism

While Sikhism proclaims all people and religions are equal in God's eyes, it also teaches reincarnation is a necessary part of spiritual evolution. A person's progress as a Sikh parallels his or her five stages of spiritual evolution. Someone in the first stage, Dharam Khand, is a Manmukh, self-centered, thinking only about the material world and oblivious to God. In the second stage, Gian Khand, the devotee becomes a Sikh, one who faithfully believes in the one immortal being and the teachings of the ten gurus, and who does not owe allegiance to any other religion besides Sikhism. Total devotion to Sikhism in the third stage, Saram Khand, means becoming initiated into the Khalsa, shedding all ego, and honoring the memory of Guru Gobind Singh through deeds and actions. In the fourth state, Karam Khand, one becomes a Gurmukh, or one who has achieved salvation and is totally God centered. The Gurmukh is thus prepared to enter the fifth stage, Such Khand, and dwell with God. For Sikhs the process of spiritual evolution and salvation begins with prayer.

Private Prayer

Prayer is very important to the Sikh faith. Sikhs must pray every day. Most Sikhs make time for morning and evening prayers. Before saying the morning prayer, many Sikhs repeat the phrase *Wahe Guru,* or "Wonderful Lord," several times. The phrase honors God, whom the Sikhs call the True Guru. The morning prayer begins with the Mul Mantra, the first words of the Guru Granth Sahib, which begins, "The One Universal Creator God. The Name is Truth."[45]

The morning prayer continues with the rest of the Japji, the original devotions of Nanak. Some Sikhs recite the entire 38 verses, which takes about twenty minutes. Some recite just the first five verses; others simply recite

Wahe Guru several times. Manmohan Singh, a member of the *gurdwara* of the Central Jersey Sikh Association in New Jersey's Washington Township, says the prayers whenever he can: "Over a period of years they become memorized. As I travel I listen to audio tapes from the holy book. There is no special recitation of prayers for specific days apart from the holy book."[46]

Most Sikhs, including this young girl, recite both morning and evening prayers.

Before sleep, Sikhs read or recite evening prayers known as the Rehras Sahib, a collection of hymns by different gurus that express praise and thanksgiving. The Guru Granth Sahib is considered the living receptacle of the True Guru and the teachings of the ten gurus. The emphasis of the Sikh holy book is its teachings and not the ten gurus who wrote it. Many Sikhs have pictures of the ten gurus displayed in their homes but these pictures are never worshipped or displayed in *gurdwaras;* at most they are used to inspire the practice of the faith and its teachings in the home.

Public Worship

Besides praying privately, Sikhs regularly visit the *gurdwara,* which literally means "door to the teachers." Most *gurdwaras* are designed or arranged like an imperial Indian court. The Guru Granth Sahib rests on a throne under a canopy and is

An Indian Sikh carries the Guru Granth Sahib during a procession at the Golden Temple. The holy text contains the teachings of the ten gurus.

treated like a living guru. Each morning *gurdwara* congregants bring the Guru Granth Sahib to the throne; each evening they retire the holy book to its bedchamber.

Specific rules dictate the manner in which worhippers enter the *gurdwara*, whose entrances are marked by a yellow and orange religious flag called the Nishan Sahib. Congregants remove their shoes and cover their heads before entering, bow before the holy book, and make offerings for the upkeep of the *gurdwara*. At Manmohan Singh's *gurdwara*, daily services begin at 4:00 A.M. and conclude at 9:00 P.M. People come into the *gurdwara* all through the day and for no fixed length of time—brief or prolonged attendance depends on the individual.

Sikhs do not have a formal clergy. Scholars and congregation members conduct worship services and perform various religious observances. In all *gurdwaras*, the Guru Granth Sahib's hymns are sung and Sikh scholars read from the text and explain it to visitors throughout the day. "People come to seek peace and recite their prayers and make their presence before the holy book," says Manmohan Singh. "You can sing along or flow with your mind or with your voice. You can close your eyes and keep listening. The idea is to do whatever you need to get the peace. I don't go to the gurdwara as an obligation to God, I go because I want to."[47] A devotee who is particularly troubled may ask for guidance from the holy book or ask for help from the True Guru. How a Sikh prays is not as important as why he or she prays. "God will understand what you are trying to say, even if you don't use words," says Manmohan Singh. "Prayer is what you sincerely speak from your heart."[48]

There is a lot of flexibility in how Sikhs worship to allow for the different cultures in the many different places Sikhs have settled. The prevailing culture Sikhs live in usually determines when Sikhs worship and what days community meals are served. For example, in Britain and the United States, most Sikhs visit their *gurdwaras* on Sunday.

Sikh Guidelines for Daily Life

In simple terms, a Sikh is a person who tries to become a good and honorable human being according to the teachings of the ten gurus. To become a good person and achieve salvation, Sikhs maintain their households, earn honest livings, and avoid worldly temptations such as alcohol, drugs, and tobacco.

A Sikh must dress simply, must always be clean, and must never pierce any parts of the body. Most Sikhs dress like those around them—in Western societies, they wear Western-style clothes. Sikh men, however, are distinguished by the turban which they wear on their head at all times.

In line with Sikh principles of equality, Sikh women will not wear a veil, which in many Indian cultures denotes secondary status. Women, like men, participate in the ceremonies at the *gurdwaras*, are initiated into the Khalsa, and become Sikh scholars.

In Sikhism a major part of devotion to God and living a good life is service to others and the community. A Sikh's voluntary service always begins at the *gurdwara*. All congregants sweep the floors of the *gurdwara*, make repairs on the building, serve water to or fan the congregation, give food to and work in the *langar*, and even dust the shoes of the people visiting a Sikh house of worship. The *gurdwaras'* communal kitchens provide Sikhs with training in voluntary service and help feed the community. Outside of working in the *gurdwara*, Sikhs are expected to serve their communities by volunteering for charitable organizations and giving generously to the poor.

Study and understanding of their faith and the writings of the ten gurus is also very important to Sikhs. Most *gurdwaras* offer classes for both adults and children to learn Gurmukhi script. Sikhs should also learn Punjabi and teach it to their children. Many Sikhs have copies of the Guru Granth Sahib in their homes. They are required to treat the holy book with the same respect and honor the same traditions surrounding its care as is done in Sikh *gurdwaras*.

While understanding and practicing their faith is of utmost importance, Sikhs do not believe in converting others to Sikhism. Instead, their role is supportive: "If you were to decide you wanted to be a Sikh and you asked me as a neighbor or friend, I would help you to understand the teachings," says Manmohan Singh. [49] Converts are accepted only in adulthood, when Sikhs believe a person is able to make his or her own choices. To further their spiritual evolution, all Sikhs are expected to work toward total devotion to their faith by becoming a member of the Khalsa. Joining the Khalsa is considered a worthy goal, but it is not necessary to join the Khalsa to be considered a Sikh.

Initiation into the Khalsa

The Khalsa, created by the tenth guru to defend the Sikh faith, is a fellowship of Sikh men and women who pledge total devotion to their faith.

Sikhs prepare food in the communal kitchen at the Golden Temple. Preparing food in communal kitchens helps prepare Sikhs for a life of community service.

Membership is not automatic; Sikhs and converts alike must meet certain conditions to undergo Sikh baptism and thereby become a member of the Khalsa.

Those wishing to join the Khalsa should be no younger than the age of eighteen, demonstrate an understanding of the principles of the faith, and must prove their devotion in daily life. Gobind Singh wrote that:

He who keeps alight the unquenchable torch of truth, and never swerves from the thought of One God; he who has full love and confidence in God and does not put his Faith, even by mistake, in fasting or the graves of Muslim Saints, Hindu crematoriums or Jogis places of sepulchre, he who recognizes the One God and no pilgrimages, alms-giving, non-destruction of life, penances or austerities; and in whose heart the light of the Perfect One shines,— he is to be recognized as a pure member of the Khalsa. [50]

Khalsa members do not eat meat, use drugs, drink alcohol, or smoke tobacco. They demonstrate their

Turban Tying Tradition

The turban is an essential article of faith. When a Sikh boy reaches adolescence, he is taken to the *gurdwara* and taught how to wear and tie his turban. The ceremony is performed in front of the Guru Granth Sahib after prayers are said. An elder member of the congregation ties the turban while family members and friends look on. It is fashioned of a single piece of fine cotton or muslin, about three feet wide and as much as fifteen feet long. The cloth is stretched, folded, rolled and gathered, and then wrapped carefully around the head in techniques that take years to master. The way a man's turban is tucked and pinched is a matter of individual preference and gives each Sikh a unique look. The turban may also be of any color. Many older Sikh men prefer to wear white turbans that reflect their acquired wisdom. Saffron and deep blue signify battle and are usually worn by Sikh warriors, and young men tend to favor bright, eye-catching shades.

A Sikh man holds one end of his long turban taut before wrapping it around his head.

commitment by wearing the five articles of faith, known as the five Ks. These articles of faith distinguish Sikhs from others; they are both marks of identification and indications of Sikh beliefs. The first of these, the *kesh*, requires that Sikhs never cut their hair or beards, a sign of spiritual consciousness and harmony with God's will. Sikh men roll and gather their hair under a turban, and Sikh women too wear turbans and/or hoods called *chunmi*. The second, the *kanga*, is a small comb keeping the hair in place, symbolizing cleanliness. The third, the *kara*, a metal bracelet worn on the wrist, binds Sikhs to the truth and restrains them from bad deeds. The fourth, the *kirpan*, is a small ceremonial dagger that reminds Sikhs to defend the truth of their faith. And the fifth, the *katcha*, is a traditional kind of underwear worn as a mark of purity.

Having understood the requirements of the Khalsa, those seeking to join must go through an initiation process or baptism modeled after the first Khalsa ceremony of 1699. Sikhs who choose to be baptized into the Khalsa must arrive at their ceremony clean, having just bathed and dressed in the five Ks. Six Khalsa members must be present to help conduct the two-hour ceremony. One of the Khalsa members explains the tenets of Sikhism and the requirements of becoming a Khalsa member. Each initiate is asked if he or she accepts these principles willingly. If affirmative responses are given, then prayers are said. Five of the Khalsa members then prepare *amrit,* or sugar water, for drinking. The water is put in a steel bowl and stirred by each Khalsa member with a double-edged sword. Each person seeking baptism is offered the *amrit* and drinks it five times from their cupped hands. The Khalsa member pouring the liquid exclaims: "Wahe guru ji ka Khalsa, wahe guru ji ki fateh!" loosely translated as "The Khalsa belongs to God, victory belongs to God!"[51] The new Khalsa members are then told they have been reborn in the guru's household and that their spiritual father is now Guru Gobind Singh, their spiritual mother is Mata Sahib Kaur, Gobind Singh's wife, and all other Khalsa members are their brothers and sisters. The men are baptized with the last name of Singh, or lion; women take the last name Kaur, which means lioness or princess. Adopting the same last name reinforces the Sikh belief in the equality of all human beings and the primacy of the Sikh family.

Marriage

The family is the cornerstone of Sikh life. Marriage joins together two adults in an equal partnership and blissful union; it also brings two families together in the Sikh community. Marriage between people under the age of eighteen, once a common practice in India, is strictly forbidden in the Sikh religion. Traditionally, parents of the bride or groom arrange Sikh marriages. But the man and woman must agree to the match for a wedding to take place. When the marriage is not arranged, the couple must seek the consent and blessings of their two families. To marry in a Sikh ceremony the couple must proclaim their belief in Sikhism and no other religion.

Sometimes the families of the couple hold a *kurmaj*, or engagement ceremony, one week before the wedding. Traditionally held at a *gurdwara* or the home of the groom's family, it is a simple ritual at which prayers are recited, hymns are sung, and *langar*, the communal meal, is served. The groom is given a *kara, kirpan,* and some Indian-style sweets. The bride's family is given an Indian suit and some sweets for the bride. If this ceremony is performed at home, the bride's family remains for a short visit at the house of the groom's family.

The Sikh marriage ceremony, or *Anand Karaj*, takes place in a *gurdwara* or at the home of the bride's or groom's parents—wherever there is a

copy of the Guru Granth Sahib. The ceremony begins with the singing of scriptural hymns. The groom enters first and, after bowing, sits in front of the Sikh holy book. The bride then joins him. A Sikh scholar gives a speech reminding the bride and groom and wedding guests of the words of the third guru: "They are not said to be husband and wife, who merely sit together. They alone are called husband and wife, who have one light in two bodies."[52] After the speech the bride's father gives the groom one end of a saffron-colored scarf, pulls the scarf over the groom's shoulder, and puts the other end in the bride's hand. Bonded by the scarf, the couple renounces all evil and declares their devotion to God. Then the couple circles the Guru Granth Sahib four times as the guests and families sing the wedding hymn "Anand," composed by the third guru, Amar Das. The fourth time around the holy book, the congregation tosses flower petals at the bride and groom. Then the entire wedding party sings more verses of "Anand" as the ceremony concludes.

In the West, Sikh weddings are only one- or two-day affairs. Most ceremonies are held in the morning followed by a celebration of dinner and dancing. Sikh weddings performed in the East are generally more

A Sikh bride wearing ornate jewelry on her hands and wrists (inset) and her husband are covered in flowers on their wedding day.

elaborate. Most are three-day affairs beginning with the groom's family and friends traveling to the bride's house in the evening. The bride's family entertains them and they spend the night at her home. The following day the ceremony is held, usually in the morning. Then the wedding party celebrates with a dinner and dancing lasting into the night. The next day the groom and his family leave with the bride to return to their home.

In line with Sikh principles of equality, Sikh women do not take their husbands' last name when they marry. Also, Sikhism forbids polygamy, the practice of marriage to more than one wife. Divorce is permitted. Traditionally, divorced men and women were discouraged from marrying another while their ex-spouse lived. Today remarrying after a divorce is more common. Widows have always been allowed to remarry in the Sikh faith.

A Sikh wedding marks the beginning of a new family. Other Sikh traditions reinforce the family's faith through life's celebrations and challenges.

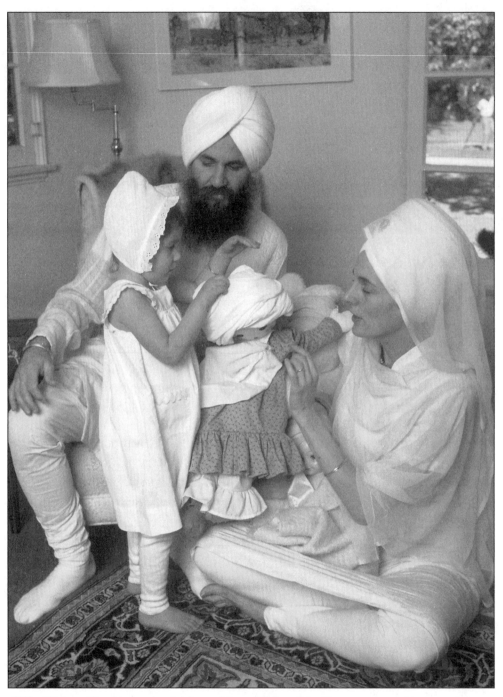

Sikh children, like this young girl dressed in traditional clothing, are named in a special ceremony created by Angad, the second Sikh guru.

Child Naming

The Sikh child-naming ceremony grew out of a story about the second guru, Angad Dev. A Sikh named Shia took his son to Angad, begging the second guru to bless the infant. Angad recited prayers and sprinkled holy water on the eyes, face, and head of the boy. He then selected one letter at random from his prayer book. Angad declared the child would now have a name beginning with that letter and ordained the ceremony for all Sikh infants in the Sikh temple.

The tradition started by the second guru continues today in *gurdwaras* all over the world. At the birth of a child, these words of Guru Arjan Dev are recited: "The True Guru has truly given a child. The long-lived one has been born to this destiny."[53] A few days later the infant is taken to the *gurdwara* for the naming ceremony, attended by relatives and friends. The parents make donations; cook and serve *karah prasad,* the sweet dough which is traditionally offered during many sacred ceremonies; and present a *rumala*, the special covering for the Guru Granth Sahib made of high-quality silk, cotton, or embroidered cloth, to the *gurdwara.*

The child-naming ceremony itself is simple. The holy book is opened and one letter is picked at random. That letter is the first in the child's name. Either the parents announce the name of the child at the ceremony or they may wait and consult with other family members, choosing the name later. At the end of the ceremony sacred sugar water is sprinkled on the baby's lips and the following prayer is recited: "The vine has grown, and shall last for many generations. The power of the Dharma [universal order] has been firmly established by the Lord. That which my mind wishes for, the True Guru has granted."[54] When the name is selected by the family, the congregation gives cheers and then the *karah prasad* is passed out and the new *rumala* is placed over the Guru Granth Sahib.

Sikh names all have special meaning. Parents choose a name for their child according to their wishes for that child. For example, "Tegh Bahadur" means brave swordsman. A child with that name would hopefully grow to be courageous. "Amar Singh" means eternal lion and "Diljit Kaur" means heart-winning lioness; according to their parents' wishes, children with these names would have strength, long life, and so on.

Traditionally, all female Sikh children are given the last name of Kaur and all male Sikh children the name of Singh. Those who later choose to join the Khalsa and go through Sikh baptism are also given these last names, so it is not possible to know a Khalsa member by name alone.

Death

Sikhs closely associate birth and death as integral parts of the continuous cycle of life. The Sikh philosophy of death is acceptance of its inevitability. Those who embrace the teachings of the ten gurus find bliss in death as it brings them closer to the supreme being. As written in the Guru Granth Sahib, "The world is afraid of death—that death fills my mind with bliss. It is only by death that perfect, supreme bliss is obtained."[55]

Because Sikhs believe in reincarnation, mourning is limited, especially for departed loved ones who have lived long, full lives. Relatives and friends recite the "Psalm of Peace," written by the fifth guru, Arjan Dev, to console themselves and the dying person. At the point of death, those close to the loved one exclaim *Wahe Guru* or "Wonderful Lord."

The funeral ceremony is often split into two different parts, the first being cremation of the body. The body is first washed and dressed in clean clothes, and in the case of baptized Sikhs, outfitted in the five articles of faith. A prayer for the salvation of the departed soul is said at the beginning of the funeral. If possible the eldest son or a close relative per-

forms the cremation. The ashes collected after cremation are usually immersed in the nearest river or sea. Some Sikh families living outside of India take the ashes to the Punjab. Monuments or headstones are never erected over the remains of the dead.

The second part of a Sikh funeral is comparable to a memorial service in which the constant reading of the entire Guru Granth Sahib provides spiritual support and consolation to the bereaved. Held at a *gurdwara* or a close relative's home, this tradition must be carried out within ten days of death. Sometimes family members perform the reading, sometimes they listen to its recitation by another *gurdwara* member. When the reading is complete, friends and relatives gather for a community meal. Often presents are given to the grandchildren of the deceased and donations to charities and religious organizations are announced at the gathering.

Holy Places

Pilgrimage has never been an integral part of the Sikh faith, but five historical *gurdwaras* have been designated as shrines, or Sikh *takhats*, meaning thrones. These holy places represent Sikh history and the importance of that history to the faith's development. Many Sikhs visit

Situated in the middle of a sacred pool, the Golden Temple is only accessible by a causeway lined with golden lanterns.

the *takhats* to better understand their beliefs and those who fought and died for those beliefs. Some 150 other *gurdwaras* have lesser degrees of historical importance.

Far more important is the most significant site in Sikhism, Sri Harmandir Sahib, the Golden Temple at Amritsar completed in 1604. The fifteen-year restoration of the Golden Temple and the surrounding complex in the late 1980s and early 1990s is a source of pride and comfort for Sikhs in the Punjab and the rest of the world. Built upon a platform in

the middle of a sacred, 500-foot long (152.4 m), 17-foot-deep (5.2 m), reflecting pool, the Golden Temple seems to rise out of the water. Unlike other religious shrines, visitors do not ascend to altars but descend stairs to an area of worship because Guru Arjan Dev designed the Golden Temple to reinforce the Sikh ideal of humility. The upper half of the building is covered in gold-plated copper sheets, giving the temple its name. The temple is surrounded on four sides by a wide marble walkway and porch; and its reflecting pool adds a quiet and peaceful quality to the place of worship surrounded by the narrow and busy streets of Amritsar. At the southern side of the temple, visitors can step down to the water of the pool. They may drink it, sprinkle it on themselves, or fill bottles with it to take with them. Many visitors collect the water for sick friends and relatives.

Akal Takht or "Throne of the Formless" is a holy temple facing the Golden Temple in Amritsar. This temple was built to house the administrative offices of the Sikh religion. Today it is used for similar purposes. Leaders of the faith have offices here and make decisions concerning *gurdwaras* worldwide. Like the Golden Temple, Akal Takht is a structure of beautiful proportions. The building is five stories high with a gold dome on its roof. Intricate carvings and wall hangings decorate the inside.

Other holy places are significant for their connection to the lives of the ten gurus. Talwandi, the birthplace of Sikhism's founder, Guru Nanak, is now known as Nanakana Sahib, a city of forty thousand in Pakistan. Nanakana Sahib has many *gurdwaras* and is a popular spot for Sikhs to visit.

Patna on the Ganges River, five hundred miles east of Delhi, is celebrated as the birthplace of the tenth

Sikh Religious Emblems

Just as the cross symbolizes Christianity and the Star of David symbolizes Judaism, important symbols are associated with Sikhism. The Khanda, shaped like a double-edged sword, symbolizes divine knowledge, its sharp edges dividing truth from falsehood. A circle around the Khanda is the Chakar, which symbolizes the perfection of the eternal God. The two-edged sword also symbolizes the importance of both temporal and spiritual authority introduced by the fifth guru Hargobind. This idea is reinforced in the Sikh teaching that Sikhs must devote time to meditation and obtaining a God-centered mind while serving human society.

The Nishan Sahib is the name given to the flag which flies outside every *gurdwara*. It is triangular, either ochre or saffron colored, and has a Khanda symbol on it.

Ik Onkar is the literal script of the first words from the Guru Granth Sahib, "There Is Only One God." Written in the Gurmukhi script, it is an attractive design that literally speaks the first tenet of Sikhism.

guru, Gobind Singh. A shrine commemorating Gobind Singh and containing relics of his life, such as his sword, four arrows, and a pair of sandals, is preserved there. Patna is also revered as the site where Guru Nanak visited and the ninth guru, Tegh Bahadur, lived. Guru Gobind Singh is also honored in the southern Indian town of Nander, where he died. A *gurdwara* housing clothes believed to be Gobind Singh's now sits on the spot where the tenth guru died. Horses supposedly descended from Gobind Singh's own steed are kept in a nearby stable.

Located in the foothills of the Himalayas, Anandpur (literally, "town of joy") is the place where the Khalsa was created and where Guru Tegh Bahadur was cremated. A shrine honoring the creation of Sikh baptism sits on the spot where Gobind Singh founded the Khalsa.

Festivals and Rites

In the earliest days of the Sikh faith, Sikhs kept many Hindu religious holidays. In an effort to differentiate Sikhism from Hinduism, Sikhs developed their own spiritual celebrations or changed the meaning of those festivals shared with Hindus. The main Sikh festivals, or *gurupurabs,* celebrate the lives of the Sikh gurus. There are ten *gurupurabs* in a calendar year; each *gurupurab* lasts three days. Sikhs celebrate with great enthusiasm, reinforcing the Sikh commitment to community service and devotion to God. Local bands play religious music and marching school children form a special part of parades organized by different *gurdwara* congregrants. Five armed guards displaying the Sikh flag escort a flower-decorated float carrying the Guru Granth Sahib through the streets. Sikhs also offer sweets and community lunches to everyone, regardless of their religious beliefs.

Four of the *gurupurabs* are considered especially important. In early January, Gobind Singh's festival celebrates the birthday of the guru who created the Khalsa, giving Sikhs a distinctive identity. Guru Arjan Dev's martyrdom day falls toward the close of May or beginning of June with parades and Sikhs serving cold sweetened milk to every passerby. The birthday of Sikhism's founder and first guru, Nanak, is celebrated in late October. Because Sikhs believe Guru Nanak brought enlightenment to the world, Nanak's festival is called Prakash Utsav, the festival of light. Guru Tegh Bahadur's martyrdom day falls at the end of November and beginning of December. During the *gurupurabs, gurdwaras* host continual readings of the Guru Granth Sahib,

Two Sikhs participate in a staged battle during a 2004 festival honoring the Sikh holy text, the Guru Granth Sahib.

lectures, and exhibits of artifacts explaining the Sikh faith.

In late November, Sikhs also mark Diwali, the Hindu Festival of Lights. The Sikh version of the celebration is called Bandi Chhorh Divas, or "the day of release of detainees," and commemorates when Guru Hargobind and other political prisoners were freed from an Islamic jail. Like Hindus, Sikhs light up their houses of worship with oil lamps and candles and shoot off fireworks outside.

Baisakhi is New Year's Day in the Punjab and is celebrated on April 13. On this day in 1699 Guru Gobind

Singh founded the Khalsa. To pay tribute to the tenth guru and the creation of the Khalsa, prayer meetings are held in *gurdwaras,* where the Guru Granth Sahib is ceremonially taken out, symbolically bathed with milk and water, and then placed back on its throne. The story of the first Khalsa members is chanted by baptized Sikhs, marching through the streets dressed in the five articles of faith.

Holla Mohalla is a Sikh festival celebrated in the spring on the day after the Hindu festival Holi, which honors the Hindu god Krishna. Started by the tenth guru, Gobind Singh, Holla Mohalla celebrates Sikh military prowess and the valor of Sikh warriors who battled the Mogul Empire. Khalsa members, dressed in traditional martial costumes, display their skill in archery, sword fencing, shooting, and bareback horse riding. They also perform mock battles and daring feats such as standing on two speeding horses.

Whether remembering spiritual leaders, bravery during oppressive times, or skills unique to their religious culture, Sikh festivals always serve the community with colorful processions and tasty food while celebrating their devotion to God and their ten gurus. Sikhs have maintained their values of community service and joyful devotion to their faith despite modern-day challenges to their religion.

chapter five

The Politics of Sikhism

In modern times Sikhism has been influenced as much by Indian politics as by the teachings of the ten gurus. Even Sikhs living outside of the Punjab have been influenced by the changes and power struggles in their faith's homeland. The political strife set in motion by partition has taken the form of calls for independent, sectarian homelands and ongoing violence between extremist Muslim, Hindu, and Sikh factions.

Religious Divisions

In the early years of independence, India's central government generally favored the Hindu majority over the country's Muslim, Christian, Buddhist, and Sikh minorities. This policy included reduced investment in one of its most productive regions, the Punjab, where substantial Sikh populations remained.

Nevertheless, the Punjab became the most prosperous state in India. Sikh farmers embraced modern methods, replacing ploughs drawn by animals with tractors and combines. As journalist M.J. Akbar writes, "The enterprise of the farmer has lifted Punjab away from the quagmire of third world proverty into at least second world comfort."[56] Largely due to the initiative of the Sikhs, the Punjab became and remains India's breadbasket and wealthiest region, with the highest

People walk through the rubble on a street in a Muslim neighborhood in Amritsar after a series of riots between extremist Hindus, Muslims, and Sikhs.

per capita income in the nation. Sikhs who left India often sent money back to relatives in the Punjab, contributing to the economic boom of the area.

Despite fostering wealth in northern India, the Sikhs still faced discrimination and oppression from a growing number of Hindu and Muslim religious extremists in the region. These fundamentalists rejected economic and democratic progress, deepening the religious divisions that had long plagued India. In a rejection of the region's moderate Hinduism, many extremist Hindus and Muslims and even some extremist Sikhs supported strict observances of their faiths and intolerance of other religions.

The worst blow to the Punjab came in 1966 when new political boundaries for India's states were drawn. Most boundaries outlined regions in which a common language was spoken. However, though Sikhs and most Hindus living in the Punjab spoke Punjabi, the Punjab was split into three different states, further reducing its political influence. Punjabis now held only 13 out of the 545 seats in India's parliament. While Sikhs did not directly blame the Punjab's Hindu majority, they did

81

Sikhs, Hindus, and Muslims

Many Sikh beliefs and practices are also found in the Hindu and Muslim faiths. There are important differences between these faiths, too. These differences have been a source of conflict in India for many years.

Sikhs and Hindus both believe in...

 Reincarnation
People experience countless cycles of birth and rebirth.

 Karma
The quality of a person's actions in this life determines the fate of the soul in the next life.

 Maya
The material world is an illusion and has many temptations that can lure people away from the religious path to salvation.

Sikhs and Hindus have different views on...

ॐ **God**
Sikhs believe in one God; Hindus worship many gods.

ॐ **Caste**
Sikhs believe all people are equal; Hindus divide society into upper and lower castes.

ॐ **Priests**
Sikhs have no priests; Hindus place great importance on their priests, known as Brahmins.

ॐ **Enlightenment**
Sikhs believe the goal of the enlightened person is to serve the community; Hindus believe the goal of the enlightened person is to become one with God.

Sikhs and Muslims both believe in...

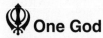 **One God**

God created heaven and earth and is all-powerful.

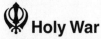 **Condemning idol worship**

The idols worshipped by the Hindus are condemned as insulting to God.

 Holy War

Holy war is justified to defend the faith.

Charity

The faithful have a religious duty to help those in need.

Sikhs and Muslims have different views on...

Salvation

Sikhs believe that people of all faiths can achieve salvation; Muslims believe that only people of the Islamic faith can achieve salvation.

Women's Role In Religion

Sikhs believe in equal participation for women in religious services; Muslims believe women cannot play a significant role in religious services.

Fasting

Sikhs do not fast as part of their religious life; Muslims fast from dawn until dusk for a month during the festival of Ramadan.

Sikhs Face Discrimination in North America

Sikh immigrants built the first *gurdwara* in North America, the Vancouver Sikh Temple, in 1908. In 1912 two more *gurdwaras* were founded, and in 1918 the Mayo Lumber Company founded by Mayo Singh built a *gurdwara* on Vancouver Island. The *gurdwara* congregants faced discrimination and ignorance of their faith from many Canadians including Mayor Beckwith of Victoria, who wrote of Sikh immigrants, "They are not suited to the country. They are immoral and quarrelsome and have not the stamina enough to become good workers. Some of them, however, make money. . . . This very success constitutes a danger." Other Canadians, like Walter W. Baer, were more open-minded. Admiring Sikh courage, faith, and tolerance, Baer wrote about the Vancouver Island *gurdwara* in the *Canadian Courier*, "The Temple cost nearly $10,000, and is a monument to religious zeal and faith of a people far from home, in a strange land which has not treated them justly." Baer particularly admired the Sikhs' "unconquerable conviction that 'God hath made of one flesh all the nations of the earth.'"

Sikhs in Vancouver, Canada, like this young boy, have been frequent targets of discrimination.

attribute their loss of political power to unjust governmental policies. Those policies, many Sikhs believed, resulted from the fear of a united Sikh state and the resentment of Sikh success. Historian Patwant Singh writes of that time:

It remains inexplicable to the Sikhs why a strong and united Punjab was viewed as a threat to the ruling party in Delhi. An increasing number attributed it to their [the Sikhs] high profile in the Indian army; their individualistic and independent temperament; their fierce pride in their religion. They also realize that Sikhism's break with its Hindu origins centuries ago continues to be viewed with disfavour by the unforgiving elements in Hindu society.[57]

Many Sikhs believed their religion was in danger of being diluted and absorbed into India's Hindu state. Some Sikhs began to sympathize with the concerns of more radical factions of the faith.

Anandpur Sahib Resolution of 1977

In 1977 the Sikh-controlled political party Akali Dal decided to take a stand concerning the treatment of the people living in the Punjab. Its president, Harchand Singh Longowal, sent a pamphlet to Prime Minister Indira Gandhi and the Indian parliament explaining Sikh concerns:

> India is a multi-lingual, multi-religious, and multi-national land. In such a land a microscopic minority like the Sikhs has genuine forebodings that, like Buddhism and Jainism earlier, they may also lose their identity in the vast ocean of the overwhelming Hindu majority.[58]

Longowal went on to say that the Sikhs had no intention of seceding from their country of origin but they did desire greater autonomy and less interference and tampering with their religious way of life.

That same year, the Akali Dal proposed the Anandpur Sahib Resolution to resolve the problems between the Punjab's Sikhs and the Indian government. This document outlined a program that gave individual Indian states more rights and say in India's government. The resolution urged that the government "recast the constitutional structure of the country on real and meaningful federal principles to obviate the possibility of any danger to national unity and the integrity of the country and further to enable the states to play a useful role for the progress and prosperity of the Indian people in their respective areas by the meaningful exercise of their powers."[59] Many thought that passing the Anandpur Sahib Resolution was an important step in maintaining India's democracy and economic stability. The distinguished Indian jurist, R.S. Narula, said, "The only way to save the country from disintegration is to accept and adopt the Anandpur Sahib Resolution for the entire country—for every state unit of India."[60]

India's leaders opposed the resolution, believing it to be the first step toward an independent Sikh state. Declaring that the proposed document threatened the unity of the nation, Prime Minister Indira Gandhi and the ruling Congress Party dismissed it. As reported in Delhi's leading newspaper, the *Hindustan Times,* the resolution amounted to a secessionist document: "Needless to say this would not only upset the Centre-State balance visualized in the Constitution but strengthen regional pull to the detriment of national unity."[61] The rejection of the resolution created further tension between ruling Hindus and Punjabi Sikhs.

Sikh Separatist Movement

The Indian government's rejection of proposals by moderate Sikhs eventually led to the growth of militant separatist Sikh groups. Many Sikhs accused Gandhi's administration and India's ruling party—headed by Giani Zail Singh, a Sikh who sided with the prime minister and later became India's president—of betraying the Sikhs. As the situation deteriorated, Gandhi took charge of the Punjab's state government, disbanding elections and administering all Punjab governmental affairs from the Indian capital in New Delhi.

Along with the loss of political power and autonomy, many Punjabi Sikhs suffered from discriminatory practices by Indian authorities. In 1982, for example, the Indian government denied many Sikhs the opportunity to attend the Ninth Annual Asian Games (an Olympics-style event). Indian soldiers stopped, searched, and forced many Sikhs traveling to Delhi for the games to return home. In the Punjab, Indian authorities unjustly arrested and imprisoned many Sikhs on mere suspicion that they were consorting with Sikh militants. Many believe the government repression in the Punjab led to what the Indian government wanted to avoid—a growing acceptance of a Sikh extremist group that wanted nothing less than secession from India and the creation of a separate Sikh state.

Many Sikh separatists responded to the political tensions by turning away from the peaceful and tolerant teachings of the faith's founder in favor of the militarism promoted by the tenth guru, Gobind Singh. In *India: A Million Mutinies Now,* V.S. Naipaul writes,

In this faith, when the world became too much for men, the religion of the 10th Guru, Guru Gobind Singh, the religion of gesture and symbol, came more easily than the philosophy and poetry of the first Guru. It was easier to go back to the formal baptismal faith of Guru Gobind Singh, to all the things that separated the believer from the rest of the world. Religion became the identification with the sufferings and persecution of the later Gurus: the call to battle. [62]

The situation came to a head in the 1980s when a Sikh group, supported by expatriates in Canada and England, called for an independent Sikh nation to be called Khalistan. The group's leader, Jarnail Singh Bhindranwale, adopted the title Sant, or Saint, to connect his actions with the teachings of the tenth guru. Martyrdom and defense of the faith by any means became the cornerstone of Bhindranwale's campaign for a separate Sikh state.

The Massacre at Amritsar

In the late 1970s and early 1980s the extremist group led by Bhindranwale manipulated the situation between Hindus and Sikhs to gain power. Abandoning the Sikh doctrine of acceptance of all faiths, Bhindranwale incited hatred between Hindus and Sikhs by desecrating Hindu temples. Under his leadership cow heads and other body parts of cows, an animal sacred to Hindus, were thrown into temples. Bhindranwale was also linked

Sikh leader Bhindranwale provoked hatred between Sikhs and Hindus and campaigned for a separate Sikh state.

to the murder of several Sikh and Hindu officials, including Amritsar police chief A.S. Atwal as he was leaving worship services in the Golden Temple. Bhindranwale believed creating more tension between the two religious groups would eventually lead to Hindus leaving the Punjab and Sikhs setting up a separate Sikh state. Eventually Bhindranwale and his small band of followers set up headquarters around the Golden Temple in Amritsar and took control of part of the Akal Takht.

On the evening of June 5, 1984, under Gandhi's orders, the Indian Army began an attack on the Amritsar complex, including the two most sacred Sikh shrines, the Golden Temple and the Akal Takht. The Golden Temple had been desecrated three times in the 1700s, but this attack would become the most serious insult in Sikh history. The carnage that resulted would divide a nation and create widespread anguish in India's Sikh communities. Officers instructed the government troops to avoid damaging the Golden Temple and the Akal Takht. One officer, Lieutenant General Dayal, who had been coming to pray at the Golden Temple since he was fourteen years old, never doubted his men would obey the orders. "The Indian army is a very religious army. Once the orders are given to them they follow them to the letter and once it was told to them [not to damage the Golden Temple] I was sure they will obey this and I am proud to say they did until the end."[63] The Indian soldiers were able to clear the Golden Temple complex, but in the end, mayhem ensued and army tanks blasted the building, killing Bhindranwale, his followers, and many innocent civilians and pilgrims.

The siege trapped several Sikh officials in other buildings of the complex. Bhan Singh, the secretary for the Shiromani Gurdwara Parbandhak Committee (SGPC), described the situation: "They cut our electricity and water supplies. It was very hot in the rooms. There was no water. We had only two plastic buckets of water. Longowal had to place two people as guards over the buckets. Many people would squeeze their undershirts to drink their sweat to quench their thirst."[64]

Others gave even more horrifying accounts. Ranbir Kaur was holed up inside the Guru Ram Das Hostel with other religious pilgrims: "We were all huddled together. We didn't know what was happening. The noise was terrifying. We had not been out of the room for more than twenty-four hours and we had no food or water. It was a very hot summer night.

I told the children that we must be ready to die. They kept on crying."[65] Many reported seeing soldiers order young Sikh men to untie their turbans, then use the turbans to tie the men's hands behind their backs before hitting them in their heads with the butts of rifles. The troops lined up many Sikh men—sometimes thirty to forty at a time—and shot them. Bhan Singh counted at least "seventy dead bodies in the compound. There were women and children too."[66]

Students at Khalsa College in Amritsar took to the streets against the attack. Some were caught up in the violence. One student, quoted by author Stephen Alter in *Amritsar to Lahore: A Journey Across the India-Pakistan Border*, told of one demonstration she witnessed, "'I remember watching from this balcony,' said Harjit, pointing in the direction of the main road. 'The police and army were lined up there and students uprooted bricks from the flowerbeds and threw them at the soldiers.'"[67]

The "White Paper on the Punjab Agitation," published in July 1984 to explain the Indian army action in the Golden Temple, attempted to reunite the different factions in the Punjab with the Indian Government: "The action which the government had had to take in the Punjab was neither against the Sikhs nor the Sikh religion; it was against terrorism and insurgency. The Sikhs are a well-integrated part of the Indian nation."[68] While most Sikhs did not side with Bhindranwale and his extremists, the attack on their holy shrine only served to increase tensions with the government. It was not long before Gandhi would pay for the government's actions with her life.

The Assassination of Indira Gandhi

On the morning of October 31, 1984, at her home in New Delhi, Indira Gandhi readied herself for a television interview. She chose a saffron-colored sari to wear to the interview, a choice that would be seen as ironic, as saffron is the color of martyrdom in Sikh tradition. As Gandhi and her assistant R.K. Dhawan approached one of the gates separating her home from her office, she smiled at Beant Singh, her Sikh bodyguard. At that point, Beant Singh drew his revolver and shot the prime minister. She fell to the ground and another Sikh bodyguard, Satwant Singh, emptied his weapon into Gandhi's body. Beant Singh put his walkie-talkie on a fence, raised his hands above his head, and reportedly said, "I have done what I had to do. Now you do what you have to do."[69] Police providing outer security for the prime minister's residence shot Beant Singh dead and wounded Satwant Singh. Gandhi's daughter-in-law Sonia rushed the gravely wounded leader to the hospital, where she was pronounced dead. She was the first Indian prime minister to be assassinated in office.

In 1984 Indian Prime Minister Indira Ghandi (foreground) was assassinated by her Sikh bodyguard.

The news of Gandhi's assassination sparked anti-Sikh riots in the immediate vicinity of the hospital. Rumors quickly spread that Sikhs rejoiced at the news of the prime minister's death and that Sikhs had also killed hundreds of railway passengers. Author Stephen Alter, who lived outside of New Delhi, writes of that time, "Within an hour or two of her assassination the news spread throughout the city, and Delhi braced itself for the inevitable violence. The streets were alive with a collective sense of anxiety and fear."[70]

The Aftermath of Assassination

Rumors and pent-up frustration over India's poor economy erupted into violence throughout the country. Author Alter describes driving home the evening of the assassination, passing barricades on the road with burning tires and groups of young men carrying makeshift weapons of crowbars, pipes, and strips of bamboo. "Our car was stopped and the rioters surrounded us, peering in through the windows. 'Don't worry,' they said, laughing and waving us past. 'It's only the Surds [Sikhs] we're looking for.' At the side of the road I saw taxis and cars in flames, their windows shattered. The Delhi police were nowhere in sight."[71]

The victims of the angry mobs were mostly Sikhs. The gathering crowd of Hindus outside the hospital where Gandhi died shouted threats to the Sikh president of India, Giani Zail Singh. The poor, who had provided cheap labor for government contractors building the venues of the 1982 Asian Games in New Delhi were now unemployed and resentful of their former bosses—many of whom were wealthy Sikhs. Rioters went looking for rich Sikhs to avenge the death of their leader and advocate. However, it was largely poor Sikhs who suffered at rioters' hands.

Two days after the assassination a group of Delhi residents came across the charred bodies of three Sikhs on the porch of a small house in a Sikh neighborhood. Many more such discoveries followed. The Indian government reported nearly three thousand people were killed in anti-Sikh riots throughout India. At the same time, many Sikhs said local Hindu residents hid them from the mobs. At the end of the hostilities, officials estimated fifty thousand Sikhs fled the chaos in the capital city for safety in the Punjab.

Many criticized India's government for its harsh handling of the situation in Amritsar. Others criticized the Delhi police for not protecting the Sikh population in the capital city and for not acting soon enough to bring those responsible for the violence to justice. The government actions and policies against the Sikhs helped militant groups gain more support.

Indira Gandhi's son Rajiv Gandhi succeeded his mother as India's prime minister. He negotiated with Sikh leaders in an effort to calm the tensions between Sikhs and the Indian government by creating the Punjab Accord that addressed the Sikhs' concerns. Still many believed the damage done could not be easily fixed.

Many fundamentalist, separatist movements publicly criticized Gandhi. Some of those, including Sikh extremists, threatened his life. He lost a bid for reelection as India's prime minister in 1989, and in 1991 he was killed by a suicide bomber in the southern Indian region of Tamil Nadu. The group responsible for the assassination, a Tamil guerrilla group fighting for a separate homeland for Tamils in Sri Lanka, had no association with any Sikh separatist group.

Sikh Militants

The violence that followed Indira Gandhi's assassination subsided, but conservative Sikhs were moved to support a growing number of militant groups. The support for Sikh militants comes from those who believe the Indian government will never treat Sikhs fairly until they have their own state of Khalistan. Supporters view the militants as staunch defenders of the religion, willing to die for their faith just as Sikh martyrs died hundred of years earlier.

Sikh militants are different from other religious militants in that they do not insist their religion replace all others. In fact, most believe they are on this earth to defend not only Sikhism but members of other persecuted faiths as well. Cynthia Keppley Mahmood writes about one Sikh militant who pointed at a portrait of the ninth guru, Tegh Bahadur, and said,

> That's Guru Tegh Bahadur. His story is so beautiful, because he sacrificed his life for the sake of another religion, for Hindus. At that time they were being persecuted by the Mughals. That's really an inspiration to me. That's why I think Sikhs are in the world, not just for Sikhs alone but for anybody who needs a Sikh. Honestly, deep in my heart I feel like our work in this world has to be much bigger than just for ourselves.

The young militant went on to say he believes his work will not be through even when or if Khalistan is established. "You have your country but

Indian police officers beat rioters in an attempt to curtail the escalating violence against Sikhs following Indira Gandhi's assassination by her Sikh bodyguard in 1984.

then you need to work on achieving justice in it and then in the rest of the world. . . . You don't get peace and justice without sacrifice and our Gurus taught us all about that."[72]

The extremism of Sikh separatists extends to religious devotion. As one Khalistani told Mahmood,

> I can tell you this not only about myself and my companions, but about all the militants I know. We wake up at three or four in the morning, bathe, and pray for hours and hours. We pray before we go on a mission, that the mission

should be successful. When we come back and it has been accomplished we thank the Guru for that. Our only mission in life is to uphold the value of dharm, righteousness. People who are fighting for that, upholding the loftiest ideals, how can they do wrong?[73]

In the years following the tragedy at Amritsar and the assassination of Indira Gandhi the Indian government has managed to control extremist Sikh movements in the Punjab and worked to negotiate compromises with the Sikh community over

93

economic and political issues. The return of peace in the Punjab and a growing economy providing more jobs for all Indians has stabilized relations between the nation's different religious factions. At the beginning of the twenty-first century, Sikh extremists continue to promote their cause but are not considered a serious threat to India's government, where Sikh representation took a significant step forward in 2004.

India's First Sikh Prime Minister

The growing economy in India has helped Sikhs, Hindus, and members of other faiths to prosper. Generally increased prosperity has helped moderate the religious tensions of the 1970s, 1980s, and early 1990s. Prominent Sikhs and Hindus who remember the strife of 1984 have come together to heal those wounds while working toward creating a stronger and more prosperous India. The June 2004 installation of India's first Sikh prime minister is an example of this cooperation.

Sonia Gandhi, the Italian-born daughter-in-law of the assassinated Indira Gandhi, was elected prime minister in the summer of 2004. However, in an effort to create more unity among the different factions in

Nearly three thousand people were killed in anti-Sikh riots after the assassination of Indira Ghandi. Here, Mother Teresa visits an area destroyed during the riots.

First Sikh Member of U.S. Congress

Dalip Singh Saund arrived in San Francisco in 1920 from a farming community in central Punjab. He earned a doctorate in mathematics from the University of California at Berkeley in 1922 and then moved to Southern California's Imperial Valley to become a farmer. In 1928 he married Marian Kosa, an American citizen who gave up her citizenship because her husband could not become a U.S. citizen under discriminatory immigration laws. When those laws were changed in 1946, Saund and his wife became U.S. citizens. His experiences led to involvement in civic activities and the local Democratic Party. In 1952 he was elected judge in Imperial County's Westmoreland Judicial District. In 1957 he was elected to the U.S. House of Representatives and served three consecutive terms in Congress. His many Sikh constituents appreciated Saund for his public service and personal understanding of their challenges in immigrating to a new nation.

India's government, Gandhi rejected the post while vowing to remain head of India's leading political party, the Congress Party. Before her surprise announcement, Gandhi asked Manmohan Singh to become India's prime minister. Manmohan Singh accepted the position, becoming the first Sikh to hold the highest office in India.

The seventy-one-year-old Manmohan Singh is a former government finance minister and known as the architect of the country's economic reforms. He has pledged to broaden economic opportunities available to the urban and rural poor. His policies reflect many of Sikhism's basic tenets: the Sikh work ethic, the importance of community service, and the tolerance of religious diversity. He has pledged to build closer alliances with other East Asian countries, and his administration reflects India's social and religious diversity. For the first time in India's history the two top posts in its government are held by members of religious minorities—Sikh Manmohan Singh as prime minister and Muslim A.P.J. Kalam as president.

Manmohan Singh values education and new technology and hopes to bring both to more of India's population by improving the country's infrastructure, including roads, power, irrigation, water supply, housing, and telecommunications.

In 2004 Manmohan Singh, pictured with his wife, became the first Sikh prime minister of India.

In his first press conference as prime minister Manmohan Singh told reporters, "The 21st century should be the Indian century."[74]

In the Punjab, Sikh voter Harbhajan Singh Puri, a retired engineer, said: "Manmohan is a brilliant man with unfaltering integrity and honesty. Sonia Gandhi will not regret her decision."[75] News reports reflect a positive opinion worldwide of the first Sikh prime minister in the world's largest democracy.

India's improving economy and infrastructure have led to more religious tolerance and understanding between groups once at odds during the chaotic days of 1984. In general, life is better for Sikhs in the Punjab. Those Sikhs who left after the violence of the 1980s and immigrated to cities in Europe, North America, and Australia expanded Guru Nanak's influence while being challenged to create a better understanding of their faith worldwide.

chapter│six

Modern Challenges for the Sikh Faith

The internal struggles in the Punjab did not destroy Sikhism; instead they strengthened the resolve of the faithful and initiated the growth of Sikhism worldwide. The Sikhs who left the Punjab to escape political and religious conflicts settled in and built other Sikh communities around the world. These Sikh immigrants continue to foster understanding of their unique faith while promoting human rights and religious freedom in their new homes.

Faith Misunderstood

Sikhs are often challenged by misperceptions of the faith. Few—other than Sikhs themselves—understand its religious tenets, and many hold the false perception that it is a militant faith. Young Sikhs, particularly in the West, face these mistaken ideas on a daily basis; some feel frustrated and unable to fit in with modern society; others see the faith as a source of strength to help them cope.

The increase in terrorist attacks by extremist religious groups has added to the misunderstanding of the Sikh faith and its followers. Particularly after the attacks on the World Trade Center on September 11, 2001, focused attention on al-Qaeda and the 2001 invasion of Afghanistan made the Taliban regime widely known, many Sikhs have been unfairly linked to terrorist organizations. The fact that male Sikhs carry small ceremonial daggers and wear turbans similar to those of Taliban members and al-Qaeda leader Osama bin Laden, only exacerbates the fears of people not familiar with Sikhism.

Tightening of international security also put Sikhs in an uncomfortable light. "Firstly, those looking for someone to attack chose not only Muslims but also Sikhs, because turbans and beards create mistaken associations with the Taliban," wrote Dominic Casciana in a *BBC News* article. "Then the [British] government caused a storm within the community by banning from airports the ceremonial Kirpan dagger, an item worn as a public statement of faith."[76]

Though the *kirpan* is not a weapon but one of the five Sikh articles of faith and a symbol of self-defense and the fight against injustice, some see it as a sign of religious militancy. Others confuse the Sikhs with modern religious extremists in light of

A Sikh man draped in an American flag participates in a candlelight vigil with other Sikhs in New York after the September 11, 2001, terrorist attacks.

Sikhs' historical militarism. However, militant Sikh separatists form only a tiny fraction of the entire modern Sikh community.

In an effort to counter the misconception and discrimination concerning their faith, many Sikhs made concerted efforts to explain their religion to government officials, educators, and the public at large. After hearing countless reports of Sikh children being verbally and physically harassed following the September 11, 2001, attacks, Parveen Kaur Dhillon of the U.S. Sikh Education Council wrote an open letter to school principals. Dhillon emphasized that there are more than half a million Sikhs, many of whom are second- and third-generation Americans, living in the United States; that Sikhs believe in the equality of humankind, service to community, and that one God unites us all; and that there is no justification for fearing Sikhs or other people who look different. Dhillon suggested developing better communication between educators and the Sikh community by creating an educational forum to promote mutual understanding and dispel irrational fears about the Sikh faith. Sikhs living in the West are not only dealing with misconceptions of non-Sikhs but with conflicts among themselves over the practice of Sikhism.

Conservative and Liberal Sikhs

There is considerable disagreement among Sikhs over how the faith and its traditions should be practiced. Assimilation and modernization has entailed controversy. More liberal Sikhs still consider anyone who accepts the teaching of the ten gurus to be a Sikh even if he or she may not follow all Sikh proscriptions against drinking alcohol, smoking tobacco, or cutting their hair. Conservative Sikhs refer to those not following all Sikh traditions as non-practicing Sikhs.

Some young Sikhs living outside the Punjab say it is difficult to maintain the unique appearance and practices of their faith. According to one Sikh Web site, third- and fourth-generation Sikhs in England and Canada "are more likely to be into drinking beer, smoking, cutting their hair,"[77] and living a non-Sikh way of life than being a practicing Sikh. Conservative Sikhs do not consider as Sikhs those who cannot live within the strict guidelines of Sikh doctrine even if they were born into the faith.

Liberal Sikh groups, especially outside of India, have mounted campaigns to unseat conservative Sikh leaders. Conservatives in turn have called for the excommunication of many liberal Sikhs and tried

A teacher instructs students in computer basics at the Khalsa Diwan School in Vancouver, Canada, the only Sikh school in North America.

to prevent other liberal Sikhs from addressing different Sikh congregations. Conflicts between conservative and liberal Sikh factions take quite specific forms, even involving the details of Sikh worship services. For example, a conflict between Canadian conservative and liberal Sikhs arose over furniture in a *gurdwara*. Traditionally, Sikhs sit on the floor during community meals to emphasize the Sikh teaching that every person is on the same level and of equal value. To many Sikhs sitting in chairs endorses elitism.

Several years ago a few Sikhs in Canada introduced tables and chairs in their *gurdwaras* because they found that the colder North American climate makes sitting on the floor uncomfortable, especially for the elderly. In some Canadian *gurdwaras,* younger members also complained about the lack of furniture. Many refused to be married in their temples if they had to sit on the floor. In 1996 conservative Sikhs called for the removal of the furniture, claiming liberal Sikhs were weakening the faith with modern practices.

In January 1997 a riot broke out at a Vancouver *gurdwara* over the issue. Several Sikhs were injured during the protest and nothing was

French Government Tries to Ban Turbans

In 2004, in an effort to avoid religious clashes and discrimination in France, the government tried to ban the wearing of all religious symbols including Sikh articles of faith. Protests against the government's move by Muslims, Jews, and Sikhs erupted all over France. Writing in support of the protesters, Roopinder Singh outlined in "Bans and Turbans," a *Tribune India* article, the importance of the turban to Sikhs and others from East India and the Middle East. "If someone talks of soiling a turban, it implies being dishonored," he wrote. Historically, wearing a turban is a sign of honor in many eastern cultures. In modern times Sikhs have been discriminated against for wearing turbans and looking different. But turbans are very much a part of Sikh identity—a symbol of the Sikh faith often representing the trials and tribulations Sikhs endured for centuries.

Many Sikhs reminded the French government that turban-wearing Sikhs fought bravely for France and the Allies in both world wars. The French government abandoned the move to ban the wearing of turbans and other religious symbols shortly after proposing it.

In 2004 Sikhs in New Delhi protest the French government's move to ban turbans and other outward religious symbols.

resolved. Eventually Sikh authorities in Amritsar ruled that the table and chairs must be removed from the Canadian temples by the middle of 1998. Still, members of several Canadian *gurdwaras* risked excommunication by vowing to keep the furniture. In December 1998, liberal candidates won management positions within a number of British Columbia *gurdwaras.* Some of those Sikh leaders called for a peacemaking conference to resolve the issue of *gurdwara* furniture once and for all. At present, the furniture remains and the *gurdwaras* retain their status as Sikh temples.

While leaders of the Sikh faith struggle to create a balance between maintaining Sikh traditions and living in the modern world, young Sikhs face personal challenges over Western culture and their faith.

Keeping Sikh Customs Alive

Many young Sikhs who in the 1990s dismissed Sikhism's religious guidelines that restrict Western practices such as drinking alcohol and cutting hair have embraced a conservative revival of religious traditions in a rejection of modern life and its stresses.

Growing up in Toronto, Canada, Jaswinder Singh was unfairly judged because he looked different. "Like most Sikhs who maintain unshorn hair, I have been harshly ridiculed, had to fight physical and verbal battles with school mates almost every day. Just trying to survive in this white-dominated culture where children were out rightly racist, was a tough daily battle."[78] Not all Sikhs longing to fit in live in the West. Robert Arnett wrote about a young Sikh in his book *India Unveiled:*

> When leaving Amritsar by train, I met a young Sikh college graduate who wanted to become a jet pilot in the Indian Air force. He informed me that many young Sikhs like himself violated religious prohibitions and trimmed their beards and cut their hair, even though it could not be seen under their turbans. He explained that it was their way of identifying with the modern world.[79]

At a December 2003 conference at the Singh Sabha Gurdwara in Slough, England, however, retired teacher Hari Singh Sewak said too many young people were turning away from their Sikh traditions. "It's alarming and this affects their life,

Traditionally, Sikh brides and grooms exchange their vows while sitting on the temple floor. Today, many young, liberal Sikhs reject this custom.

their parents and will affect future generations as well as the Sikh faith," Sewak said. "Sikhism does not look to convert people, so losing your own people has a significant impact."[80]

The 2003 film *Bend It Like Beckham* dramatizes the challenges of following both Sikhism and Western customs. Set in Great Britain, the movie is about a young woman who defies her family's wishes to play soccer on a professional girls' team. She becomes romantically involved with the male coach of her team, a non-Sikh of Irish descent. Other Sikh characters also struggle with maintaining their faith's traditions in the modern world. For

example, most of the young male Sikhs in the film cut their hair and do not wear turbans, viewing such customs as old-fashioned and contrary to modern-day life.

Another problem young Sikhs face—especially those living outside of India—is not understanding the language of their faith. "I was in my parents' gurdwara over the holidays and I don't think I understood even 10 percent of what was said. This is due to my inadequate understanding of Punjabi,"[81] one Sikh youth remarks. Busy Sikh parents in Britain and North America have little time to teach their children a language they only hear in their *gurdwara.* According to an article by Sikh scholar Amir Tuteja, "The inadequate knowledge of Punjabi stems probably from the fact that parents don't put an effort to speak Punjabi at home . . . especially when their kids are young. Many parents and children say that because they spend the better part of the day around the English speaking people, they don't get a chance to speak Punjabi."[82] Some *gurdwaras* conduct worship services in English so young members can understand their religion better. Many Sikh leaders from around the world are beginning to reach out to Sikh youth by providing more and better programs teaching them about their faith, its language, and its history. Often it is the knowledge of Sikh history that strengthens the faith and beliefs of Sikh youth.

Assimilation in Modern Times

While not always evidenced by outward appearances, most Sikhs claim their faith is uniquely suited to modern life. Sikhism has been described as both modern and rational in that it does not foster blind faith nor encourage meaningless ritual. Sikhism's founder Guru Nanak rejected most of the superstitious practices of his time

and promoted a philosophy of self-reliance and service to others. It is this self-reliance and dedication that has fostered the economic success of Sikhs. As Robert Arnett writes in *India Unveiled,* "The Sikhs place great emphasis on the work ethic. As a result of their toil, the Punjab is the most developed agricultural state in India today. These successes can be largely attributed to their industriousness, as other areas of India have land as fertile."[83] Writer Jaswinder Singh agrees, noting that Sikhism builds character—especially the kind of character needed for financial success in an increasingly competitive world. "It [Sikhism] tells its followers to be 'hard workers' to earn their daily bread,"[84] writes Singh in an article on a Sikh Web site. Sikh teachings stress self-reliance in all aspects of life. Sikhs have always supported their faith by paying for and working at their own *gurdwaras.*

Gaining knowledge is another important tenet of Sikhism. "Sikhism is an intellectual way of life," writes Jaswinder Singh. "Sikhs are told very strongly, explicitly to seek knowledge within the Guru Granth Sahib. Knowledge is the key to enlightenment."[85] In their pursuit of knowledge many Sikh entrepreneurs have embraced new technologies, successfully creating and developing new

English in the Gurdwara

Conservative and liberal Sikhs have long debated whether or not to provide English-language worship services in Sikh *gurdwaras* located in English-speaking countries. Many young Sikhs and Sikh converts living outside the Punjab do not understand Punjabi well enough to read Sikh scripture. Teja Singh of Khalsa College, Amritsar, describes this problem in the following way: "As long as Sikhism had to deal with people whose language was akin to Punjabi or Hindi, it had all possibilities of advance. But as soon as it came in contact with people who could not be approached in the original language of the Sikh Scriptures, the attempt failed." Providing English-speaking worship services would help many Sikhs practice their faith. However, conservative Sikhs question whether the English language could do justice to Sikh scriptures. Both conservative and liberal Sikhs agree that more classes and programs teaching Punjabi should be available for Sikhs everywhere.

Sikh scripture is written in Punjabi, a language that few Sikhs outside the Punjab understand.

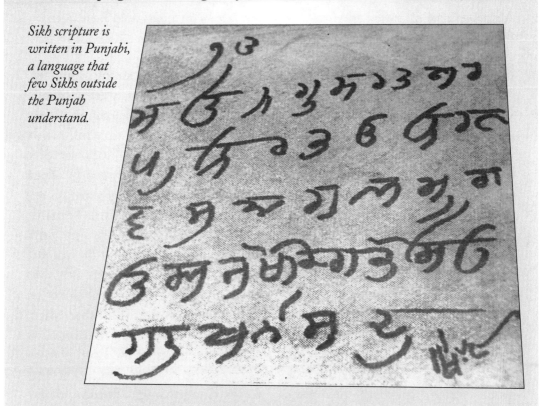

105

Most Sikhs pride themselves on a strong work ethic. Here, a Sikh sells clothes out of a store located in the part of Toronto known as Little India.

businesses. Their military service has brought them to many areas of the world, exposing them to new ideas and cultures. These experiences provide Sikhs with more insight into business and the growing global economy.

Many claim Sikhism is particularly well suited to the condition of modern society because it supports democracy. According to Sikh philosophy, "the welfare of man is best secured by elected representatives. This principle is the guiding rule of the Khalsa."[86] Rejecting caste and other delineations of social and religious status, Sikhism promotes equality and the right of all people to

make decisions concerning their lives. In his article "My Thirteen Reasons for Sikhism" Jaswinder Singh writes that Sikhism is compatible with democracy because it "does not look down upon people who follow other religions [by considering them] 'inferior, non-believer'" and because Sikhism is a religion "stressing 'universal equality' amongst all human beings."[87]

Another progressive Sikh doctrine demands that the faithful share their success. "To share this with others, as well as to remember the Lord in their heart" is the goal of Sikhs, according to Jaswinder Singh. "Hence within Sikhism, there is compassion towards all of humanity, a fact of social reform."[88] People from any religion or culture can come to any Sikh worship service or holy place, without restriction.

> [Visitors] are served in the Gurdwara . . . kitchen with the same dignity as if they were Sikhs. They are allowed to participate in Singing Hymns . . . even if they are not Sikhs. They are allowed to read the Guru Granth Sahib Ji (if they know how to read Gurmukhi Script) even if they are not Sikhs. They are allowed to discuss Sikhism in these places of worship even if they are not Sikhs.[89]

Sharing and social reform are two of the ways Sikhs continue to improve the modern world in which they live.

Sikhs in Britain

The largest Sikh community outside of the Punjab is in Great Britain, where approximately 750,000 Sikhs live. More than 400,000 Sikhs live in London alone. Most British Sikhs immigrated to Great Britain in the 1950s and 1960s after serving in the British military. Britain's Sikh community showed their strength and pride during the three hundredth anniversary of the founding of the Khalsa commemorated on April 14,

1999. In Birmingham alone, 60,000 Sikhs took part in parades and programs celebrating the founding of their faith.

Sikhs live and work in all parts of Britain. Most Sikhs came to Britain to pursue jobs and careers. Many found work in the British transportation industry after reading about opportunities with companies like London Transport. Others sought to further their education to become doctors, lawyers, engineers, and teachers.

The road to acceptance has been long and bumpy for British Sikhs, but they have successfully fought for their rights while educating others about their faith. Sikhs worked to pass legislation protecting their right to wear turbans. Now Sikhs are exempt from wearing helmets on motorcycles and other headgear in professions like the police force, bus service, and the fire brigade, because helmets cannot fit over their turbans.

In 2003 British Sikhs gathered together at a conference to establish their own political party, hoping to make their concerns known to the British government. "What we want to do is create local ownership of these issues so we can get more Sikhs involved in mainstream politics,"[90] said Dabinderjit Singh, spokesman for the Sikh Secretariat. According to the 2001 census, 40 percent of the Sikhs living in Britain are under the age of twenty-four. Dabinderjit Singh and others at the conference want to get young Sikhs involved in politics "so that when the local MP (politician) comes to speak at the Gurdwara at election time, they perhaps get a few awkward questions rather than simply rolling out the red carpet."[91]

Perhaps the best way to foster understanding of Sikhism in Britain is what British Sikhs have traditionally done—opened *gurdwaras* and welcomed visitors. The first *gurdwara* in Britain opened in 1911 in Putney. Today there are more than one hundred *gurdwaras* in the United Kingdom. The newest one is second in size and importance only to the Golden Temple in Amritsar, India. The Sri Guru Singh Sabha, located in Southall, cost 17 million British pounds to build. The temple has a golden dome of pure gold leaf, a dining hall that can serve five hundred people, a library, seminar room, and a prayer hall that can accommodate up to twenty-five hundred worshippers.

Canadian Sikhs

The century-old Sikh community in Canada is the oldest and largest in North America. Some of the first Sikhs to immigrate to Canada were Punjabi soldiers from British Hong Kong regiments that traveled through British Columbia during Queen Victoria's Diamond Jubilee Celebration in 1897. This part of Canada reminded them of their home with its comfortable climate and rich farmland. Encouraged by the stories of their colleagues, many Punjabis who served in the British army came to western Canada. Of the nearly five thousand East Indians who settled in Canada by 1907, more than 98 percent were Sikhs retired from the British military. By the 1950s Sikhs made up more than 85 percent of all East Indian immigration to Canada.

Canadian Sikhs also faced discrimination as well as some regressive immigration laws. In 1907 more than twenty-five hundred Sikhs immigrated to Canada. Under the continuous journey law passed in 1908, only six Sikhs were allowed to immigrate to Canada annually. The law was part of a plan to send back the five thousand Sikhs who came to Canada by not allowing male Sikh immigrants to send for their wives and children. During the summer of 1911 the first Sikh women to come to Canada were the wife and daughter of a Vancouver Sikh, Hira Singh. At the docks, Canadian authorities arrested both Hira Singh's wife and daughter and held them for deportation. "By

HENDERSON LIBRARIES

Check Out Receipt

Green Valley Library
702-207-4260
hendersonlibraries.com

Tuesday, July 31, 2018 11:43:24 AM

Title: Bikkiism
Material: book
Due: 08/21/2018

Total items: 1

You just saved $29.95 by using your library.

Thank you for using Henderson Libraries!

Manage your account online @
HendersonLibraries.com

HENDERSON LIBRARIES

Check Out Receipt

Green Valley Library
702-207-4560

Tuesday ... 11:43:14 AM

total items: 1

You just saved $24.95 by ... library

Thank you for using ...

Manage your account online @
ndersonlibraries.com

denying Sikhs their wives and children it was hoped that within a few years most of the Sikhs in Canada would return to their homeland," writes Sandeep Singh Brar. "Between 1904 and 1920 only nine women were allowed to immigrate to Canada."[92] Despite the Canadian government's discriminatory policies, Sikh immigrants remained steadfast. Most had dedicated their lives to serving the British Empire and felt they deserved all the rights given other British Empire citizens in Canada. Many Canadian Sikhs destroyed their British military uniforms and medals in protest and frustration of their treatment in Canada. Eventually the laws were changed and the Canadian Sikhs made a concerted effort to proudly practice their religion, holding religious parades in the streets and working to explain their beliefs to other Canadians.

Sikhs in Vancouver, Canada, watch as two men clash in a staged fight during a 2004 festival celebrating the Sikh faith.

A Sikh family relaxes outside their home in Espanola, New Mexico, where many Sikhs have settled.

In recent years Canadian Sikhs have successfully fought for their rights to practice their religion. For example, a Quebec school board banned a twelve-year-old Sikh boy from wearing his ceremonial dagger or *kirpan* to school. The school board considered the small blunt metal dagger a weapon. Quebec's Sikh community maintained school officials failed to understand the importance of the *kirpan* to their beliefs. "Quebec's education policy has failed to keep up with the new reality of cultures arriving in the province,"[93] said Manjit Singh, director of the Canadian Sikh Council. A Quebec court ruled in favor of the boy's right to wear the *kirpan* to school.

Sikhs in the United States

In the early 1900s many Sikhs moved south from Canada to the United States. Unfortunately, Sikhs coming to the United States faced discriminatory immigration laws similar to those in Canada. Still the Sikhs persisted and the first *gurdwara* in the United States was built in Stockton, California, in 1915. Many Sikhs became farmers in fertile valleys around Stockton and in the middle of the state. By the end of World War II the immigration laws of the United States changed again, allowing for more East Indian immigrants. Today there are an estimated 150,000 Sikhs living in communities across the United States.

Many Sikhs are coming to the United States in search of higher education. Most of the approximately four hundred Sikh families living in the Durham, North Carolina, area settled there to attend or work in one of three major universities in what is known as the Research Triangle. Members of this Sikh community include doctors, engineers, and computer specialists. As North Carolina's Sikh community grows, its members feel an obligation to educate their children and others about their faith. "When we came here in the 1970s, we were focused on doing things for ourselves," says Inderdeep Chatrath, a federal compliance officer at Duke University's Department of Institution Equity. "Now we see we are responsible for carrying this forward. We need to make a greater commitment to our children."[94]

Sikhs in other universities have found a positive way of educating the public about their faith through the development of Sikh studies programs. In 1977 the University of California at Berkeley established a program teaching Sikh studies and the Punjabi language. In the late 1980s Columbia University in New York City and the University of Michigan also began community-sponsored programs in Sikh studies. Like their counterparts in Europe and Canada, many Sikh children in the United States face ridicule and prejudice for their beliefs, but most Sikhs say this harassment fades away as they mature. Wearing a turban is much easier for Sandeep Singh Caberwal now that he is in college. "You explain it's part of your religion—part of your identity," says Caberwal, a sophomore at Duke University. "On college campuses people accept almost anything."[95] Community involvement, education, and social reform are all ways in which Sikhs practice their faith and help others understand it. That understanding is especially important for those Sikhs living outside the Punjab and struggling with cultures different from their own.

Strengthening the Faith

Since Guru Nanak founded Sikhism, Sikhs have set spiritual examples for potential converts, defended their beliefs and the beliefs of others, and faced ridicule from many ignorant of their faith. The struggle to maintain that faith continues today. Young Sikhs especially find it difficult to fit in with their non-Sikh peers. Sikh parents need support to teach their children Punjabi, Sikh history, and the meaning of many Sikh practices. The extent of that support often determines whether their children will accept or reject Sikh traditions. Being a young Sikh in a modern culture where the Sikh faith is not understood certainly is not easy. Many Sikhs believe the key to this dilemma is education—both of Sikhs and the non-Sikh public.

Many Sikh congregations are providing programs to teach their young Punjabi and Sikh history. Members of the Singh Sabha Gurdwara in Slough, England, intend their Sikh school to pass on Sikh heritage, traditions, and especially the Punjabi language that is vital to understanding Sikh scriptures.

Other Sikhs reach out to the larger community through political involvement—bringing to light issues important to members of the faith and helping non-Sikhs in the political arena better understand Sikhism. Some Sikhs reach out through community service. In 2003 the Sikh Community Care Project and the Central Gurdwara Singh Sabha in Glasgow, Scotland, were given the Queen's Award for Voluntary Service. Both organizations are active in their communities while providing information about Sikhism. Sikhs have a long history of helping others through community service. When the first *gurdwara* established in the United States opened in Stockton, California,

A Sikh woman plays cards with her father and grandfather in her California home. Pictures of Sikh gurus hang on her wall as testament to her faith.

in 1915, its members immediately took it upon themselves to assist the poor and downtrodden. Patwant Singh writes in his book *The Sikhs*, "Charity was practiced by the members and no man applying for shelter or food was ever turned away, regardless of who he was. The hobos passing by on the Southern Pacific tracks, just behind the Temple, would always be fed from a kitchen dining room, and a dormitory located on the ground floor would provide sleeping quarters."[96]

The challenges facing the Sikh faith are many and some seem daunting. Yet while Sikhism has not gained a lot of converts in the last twenty years, they have not lost many followers; the number of Sikhs worldwide has remained constant. As Iqbal Singh, a Sikh professor of international relations at Duke University, says, "It's a Sikh trait to take up a challenge. Life is adversity. We teach that the greater the struggle, the more proficient you are at handling challenges."[97] Most young Sikhs find comfort in their faith. They take pride in the history of its gurus, saints, and leaders. "The people who founded our religion fought so hard to make it what it is today," says Tina Singh, a senior at Cary High School in Durham, North Carolina. "It's awesome to see how they persevered and stood up for their rights."[98] Jasjit Singh recalls he realized the strength of his faith when he was in college. "A religion that was born in such tumultuous times could only survive by being strong and powerful," Jasjit Singh writes. "And then came the realization that I was a Sikh. I was the one who would protect the weak and serve the poor. I was the one who would fight for the oppressed. And I had been given the power to do so."[99]

As Sikhism expands beyond its birthplace in the Punjab, more Sikh leaders have begun to promote understanding and acceptance of their faith. Whether through charity, educational programs, or simply the enthusiastic celebrations of Sikh festivals, the followers of Sikhism demonstrate the humanity behind the faith. It is the Sikhs' willingness to reach out to others which best defines the teachings of Guru Nanak, Sikhism's founder.

Notes

Introduction: Who Are the Sikhs?

1. Guru Granth Sahib, Mul Mantra, 1:1. Trans. SearchGurbani.com, www.searchgurbani.com.
2. Quoted in Yonat Shimron, "Sikh(ing) Challenges," Sikhs in England Home Page, 2004. www.sikhs.org.uk.
3. Quoted in Rebecca Laird, "A Visit to the Sikh Gurdwara," *Sacred Journey: The Journal of Fellowship in Prayer,* February 2002.

Chapter 1: The Origins of Sikhism

4. Quoted in Patwant Singh, *The Sikhs.* New York: Doubleday, 2001, p. 19.
5. Patwant Singh, *The Sikhs,* p. 19.
6. Guru Granth Sahib, Asa 471:2.
7. Guru Granth Sahib, Japji 4:14.
8. Guru Granth Sahib, Maajh 140:18.
9. Guru Granth Sahib, Asa 9:15.
10. Guru Granth Sahib, Rag Bhairon 1136:11.
11. Khushwant Singh, *A History of the Sikhs: Volume 1: 1469–1838.* New Delhi: Oxford University Press, 1999, p. 31.
12. Guru Granth Sahib, Japji 1:3
13. Guru Granth Sahib, Maajh 141:11.
14. Guru Granth Sahib, Asa 473:8–10.
15. Quoted in Patwant Singh, *The Sikhs,* p. 24.
16. Quoted in Sandeep Singh Brar, "The First Master: Guru Nanak Dev (1469–1536)," *Sikhism.* www.sikhs.org/guru1.htm.
17. Joseph Davey Cunningham, *A History of the Sikh People: From the Origins of the Nation to the Battles of the Sutlej.* Delhi: S. Chand, 1966, p. 34.

Chapter 2: The Gurus and Development of Sikh Beliefs

18. Quoted in Sandeep Singh Brar, "The Third Master: Guru Amar Das (1479–1574)," *Sikhism.* www.sikhs.org/guru3.htm.
19. Guru Granth Sahib, Raga Jaijaiwanti 429: 12–13.
20. Quoted in Sandeep Singh Brar, "The Fourth Master: Guru Ram Das (1534–1581)," *Sikhism.* www.sikhs.org/guru4.htm.
21. Quoted in *All About Sikhs,* "What Is Karma?" www.allaboutsikhs.com/mansukh/042.htm.
22. Quoted in Sandeep Singh Brar, "The Fifth Master," *Sikhism,* www.sikhs.org/guru5.htm.
23. Quoted in Sandeep Singh Brar, "The Tenth Master," *Sikhism,* www.sikhs.org/guru10.htm.
24. Quoted in *All About Sikhs,* www.allaboutsikhs.com/gurus/guruarjan.htm, p.2.
25. Quoted in *All About Sikhs,* www.allaboutsikhs.com/gurus/gurugobind.htm, p. 1.
26. Quoted in Brar, "The Fourth Master."
27. Guru Granth Sahib, Rag Bhairon, 1128:1–2.
28. Quoted in Patwant Singh, *The Golden Temple.* Delhi: Time Books International, 1988, p. 37.
29. Quoted in Khushwant Singh, *A History of the Sikhs,* p. 60.
30. Quoted in Khushwant Singh, *A History of the Sikhs,* p. 77.

31. Quoted in Khushwant Singh, *A History of the Sikhs,* p. 77.
32. Quoted in Khushwant Singh, *A History of the Sikhs,* p. 90.

Chapter 3: Building an Empire

33. Quoted in Ganda Singh, *Life of Banda Singh Bahadur,* Patiala: Punjabi University Press, 1990, pp. 19–20.
34. Quoted in Patwant Singh, *The Sikhs,* p. 104.
35. John Keay, *India: A History.* New York: Atlantic Monthly, 2000, p. 411.
36. Quoted in K.S. Duggal, *Ranjit Singh: A Secular Sikh Sovereign.* Delhi: Abhinav, 1989, p. 47.
37. Quoted in Bawa Satinder Singh, ed., *My Indian Peregrinations: The Private Letters of Charles Stewart Harbinge, 1844–1847.* Lubbock: Texas Tech University Press, 2001, p. 150.
38. Quoted in Patwant Singh, *The Sikhs,* p. 168.
39. Quoted in Patwant Singh, *The Sikhs,* p. 175.
40. Quoted in Mark Tully and Satish Jacob, *Amritsar: Mrs. Gandhi's Last Battle.* London: Jonathan Cape, 1986, p. 32.
41. Quoted in Jawaharlal Nehru, *An Autobiography.* Delhi: Jawaharlal Nehru Memorial Fund, 1980, pp. 175–76.
42. Khushwant Singh, *A History of the Sikhs, Volume 2: 1839–1974.* Oxford: Oxford University Press, 1977, pp. 112–13.
43. Alan Campbell-Johnson, *Mission with Mountbatten.* London: Robert Hale, 1952, p. 79.
44. Quoted in Tully and Jacob, *Amritsar,* pp. 38–39.

Chapter 4: The Practices and Traditions of Sikhism

45. Guru Granth Sahib 1:1.
46. Quoted in Laird, "A Visit to the Sikh Gurdwara," p. 13.
47. Quoted in Laird, "A Visit to the Sikh Gurdwara," p. 10.
48. Quoted in Laird, "A Visit to the Sikh Gurdwara," p. 14.
49. Quoted in Laird, "A Visit to the Sikh Gurdwara," p. 11.
50. Quoted in Sandeep Singh Brar, "The Khalsa," *Sikhism.* www.sikhs.org/khalsa.htm.
51. Brar, "The Khalsa."
52. Guru Granth Sahib, Soohee 788: 11–12.
53. Guru Granth Sahib, Asa 396:2.
54. Guru Granth Sahib, Asa 396:5–6.
55. Guru Granth Sahib, Salok 1365: 12–13.

Chapter 5: The Politics of Sikhism

56. Quoted in Tully and Jacob, *Amritsar,* p. 36.
57. Patwant Singh, *The Sikhs,* p. 207.
58. Quoted in Tully and Jacob, *Amritsar,* p. 51.
59. Quoted in Patwant Singh, *The Sikhs,* p. 211.
60. Quoted in Patwant Singh, *The Sikhs,* p. 211.
61. Quoted in Patwant Singh, *The Sikhs,* p. 211.
62. V.S. Naipaul, *India: A Million Mutinies Now.* Delhi: Rupa, 1990, p. 450.
63. Quoted in Tully and Jacob, *Amritsar,* p. 158.
64. Quoted in Tully and Jacob, *Amritsar,* p. 169.

65. Quoted in Tully and Jacob, *Amritsar,* p. 171.
66. Quoted in Tully and Jacob, *Amritsar,* p. 170.
67. Stephen Alter, *Amritsar to Lahore: A Journey Across the India-Pakistan Border.* Philadelphia: University of Pennsylvania Press, 2001, p. 52.
68. Quoted in Tully and Jacob, *Amritsar,* p. 212.
69. Quoted in Tully and Jacob, *Amritsar,* p. 2.
70. Alter, *Amritsar to Lahore,* p. 13.
71. Alter, *Amritsar to Lahore,* p. 13.
72. Cynthia Keppley Mahmood, *Fighting for Faith and Nation: Dialogues with Sikh Militants.* Philadelphia: University of Pennsylvania Press, 1996, p. 42.
73. Mahmood, *Fighting for Faith and Nation,* p. 47.
74. *BBC News/South Asia,* "India Set for New Prime Minister," June 9, 2004. newsvote.bbc.co.uk/south_asia.stm.
75. *BBC News/South Asia.* "India Set for New Prime Minister."

Chapter 6: Modern Challenges for the Sikh Faith

76. Quoted in Dominic Casciana, "British Sikhs Find Voice in Political Party," *BBC News,* September 13, 2003. newsvote.bbc.co.uk.
77. Jaswinder Singh, "My Thirteen Reasons for Sikhism," *Sikhism.* www.sikhs.org/art4.htm.
78. Jaswinder Singh, "Why Sikhism?" *Sikhism.* www.sikhs.org/art3.htm.
79. Robert Arnett, *India Unveiled.* Columbus, GA: Atman, 1996, p. 72.
80. Jaswinder Singh, "Why Sikhism?"
81. Quoted in Amir Tuteja, "Use of English in Gurdwaras," *Sikhism.* www.sikhs.org/art6.htm.
82. Quoted in Tuteja, "Use of English in Gurdwaras."
83. Arnett, *India Unveiled,* p. 72.
84. Jaswinder Singh, "My Thirteen Reasons for Sikhism."
85. Jaswinder Singh, "My Thirteen Reasons for Sikhism."
86. Quoted in *All About Sikhs,* "Is Sikhism Suited to the Conditions of Modern Society?" www.allabout sikhs.com.
87. Jaswinder Singh, "My Thirteen Reasons for Sikhism."
88. Jaswinder Singh, "My Thirteen Reasons for Sikhism."
89. Jaswinder Singh, "My Thirteen Reasons for Sikhism."
90. Quoted in Casciana, "British Sikhs Find Voice in Political Party."
91. Quoted in Casciana, "British Sikhs Find Voice in Political Party."
92. Sandeep Singh Brar, "Century of Struggle and Success: The Sikh Canadian Experience," *Sikhism.* www.sikhs.org/100th/part2a.html.
93. Quoted in Mike Fox, "Sikh Wins Right to Wear Dagger," *BBC News,* May 18, 2002. news.bbc.co.uk.
94. Quoted in Shimron, "Sikh(ing) Challenges."
95. Quoted in Shimron, "Sikh(ing) Challenges."
96. Patwant Singh, *The Sikhs,* p. 242.
97. Quoted in Shimron, "Sikh(ing) Challenges."
98. Quoted in Shimron, "Sikh(ing) Challenges."
99. Jasjit Singh, "On Being a Sikh," *Sikhism.* www.sikhs.org/art7.htm.

For Further Reading

Olivia Bennett, *A Sikh Wedding*. London: Hamilton, 1985. With lots of colorful photographs and personal interviews, this book depicts the Sikh marriage ceremony and the celebrations surrounding it.

Kerry Brown, *Sikh Art and Literature*. London: Routledge, 1999. This book was published with the cooperation of the Sikh Foundation. By presenting and discussing many Sikh works, including those which depict the diversity of the Punjab as an influence and the heroics of Sikh saints and soldiers, it chronicles how Sikh culture mirrored the growth and development of the Sikh faith.

John Coutts, *Sikh Festivals*. Chicago: Heinemann Library, 1997. This book introduces Sikh celebrations through interviews with Sikh children on their religious lives.

Karwaljit Kaur-Singh, *Sikh Gurdwara*. Milwaukee: Gareth Stevens, 2000. Children's book which gives an overview of the best-known and most beautiful Sikh places of worship.

Victoria Parker, *The Golden Temple: And Other Sikh Holy Places*. Chicago: Heinemann Library, 2003. Provides information and photos on the most important Sikh place of worship.

John F. Richards, *The Mughal Empire: The New Cambridge History of India*. Cambridge: Cambridge University Press. Provides a comprehensive history of India from the time of the founding of the Sikh faith to British colonial rule.

Web Sites

All About Sikhs (www.allaboutsikhs.com). Gives an overview of the religion and provides many links to its history, symbols, and views of practicing Sikhs on their religion.

Religious Tolerance.org (www.religious tolerance.org). This Web site offers an overview of Sikhism as well as other religions and discusses the importance of religious education.

The Sikhism Home Page (www.sikhs.org/topics.htm). Provides information on the history of Sikhism, the lives of the ten gurus, Sikh symbols, and articles by modern-day Sikhs on their faith.

Works Consulted

Books

Stephen Alter, *Amritsar to Lahore: A Journey Across the India-Pakistan Border*. Philadelphia: University of Pennsylvania Press, 2001. Alter provides an in-depth discussion of the conflicts surrounding the India-Pakistan border including the dislocation of Pakistan's Sikhs and the intolerance they faced when immigrating to India.

Robert Arnett, *India Unveiled*. Columbus, GA: Atman, 1996. A book written from a personal perspective by a man who has traveled extensively through India. Includes many beautiful photographs.

Alan Campbell-Johnson, *Mission with Mountbatten*. London: Robert Hale, 1952. This book provides firsthand observations by British military personnel of Sikh rebellions and protests.

Joseph Davey Cunningham, *A History of the Sikh People: From the Origins of the Nation to the Battles of the Sutlej*. Delhi: S. Chand, 1966. A new edition of Cunningham's book about the Sikhs. The author had firsthand knowledge of the Sikh Empire, having befriended and traveled with Maharaja Ranjit Singh.

K.S. Duggal, *Ranjit Singh: A Secular Sikh Sovereign*. Delhi: Abhinav, 1989. A comprehensive biography of the leader of the Sikh Empire.

John Keay, *India: A History*. New York: Atlantic Monthly, 2000. An overall view of Indian history including references to the Sikhs.

Cynthia Keppley Mahmood, *Fighting for Faith and Nation: Dialogues with Sikh Militants*. Philadelphia: University of Pennsylvania Press, 1996. A balanced report on the motivations, beliefs, and strategies of Sikh militants.

Gurinder Singh Mann, Paul David Numrich, and Raymond B. Williams, *Buddhists, Hindus, and Sikhs in America*. Oxford: Oxford University Press, 2001. An excellent book on Sikh immigration to the West written from the personal perspectives of many East Asian immigrants.

Philip Mason, *A Matter of Honour: An Account of the Indian Army, Its Officers and Men*. London: Jonathan Cape, 1974. A comprehensive history of the Indian army from its inception in the late 1940s.

V.S. Naipaul, *India: A Million Mutinies Now*. Delhi; Rupa, 1990. Includes an account of Sikh struggles after Indian independence.

Jawaharlal Nehru, *An Autobiography*. Delhi: Jawaharlal Nehru Memorial Fund, 1980. The view of India's independence and early days from the perspective of its first prime minister, Jawaharlal Nehru.

Bawa Satinder Singh, ed., *My Indian Peregrinations: The Private Letters of Charles Stewart Harbinge, 1844–1847*. Lubbock: Texas Tech University Press, 2001. A collection of correspondence to and from a British governor-general of India.

Ganda Singh, *Life of Banda Singh Bahadur*. Patiala: Punjabi University Press, 1990. A biography of the seventeenth-century

Sikh king who went to war against the Moghul rulers of India.

Kushwant Singh, *A History of the Sikhs: Volume 1: 1469–1839.* New Delhi: Oxford University Press, 1999. A comprehensive view of Sikh history with an emphasis on the teachings of the ten gurus.

———, *A History of the Sikhs, Volume 2: 1839–1974.* Oxford: Oxford University Press, 1977. The continuation of the author's first history of the Sikhs including detailed accounts of the Sikh Empire and India's independence movement.

Nikky-Guninder Kaur Singh, *Sikhism: World Religions.* New York: Facts On File, 1993. A comprehensive overview of the Sikh faith, its history, practices, and people.

Patwant Singh, *The Golden Temple.* Delhi: Time Books International, 1988. A Sikh scholar's insight into the history and meaning of the spiritual center of the Sikh faith.

———, *The Sikhs.* New York: Doubleday, 2001. An excellent overview of the history of the spiritual, political, and social history of the Sikhs, providing insight into the challenges Sikhs face in the modern world.

Narendre K. Sinha, *Ranjit Singh.* Calcutta: A. Mukherjee, 1960. A new edition of a 1933 biography of the founder and leader of the Sikh Empire.

Ian Talbot, *Punjab and the Raj: 1849–1947.* Delhi: Manohar, 1988. A book that examines Sikh influence from the time of Ranjit Singh until India gained independence from the British.

Mark Tully and Satish Jacob, *Amritsar: Mrs. Gandhi's Last Battle.* London: Jonathan Cape, 1986. A comprehensive and early account of the Indian army's storming of the Sikh temple at Amritsar and the assassination of Indira Gandhi.

Periodicals

Rebecca Laird, "A Visit to the Sikh Gurdwara," *Sacred Journey: The Journal of Fellowship in Prayer,* February, 2002.

Internet Sources

All About Sikhs, "Is Sikhism Suited to the Conditions of Modern Society?" www.allaboutsikhs.com.

———, "What Is Karma?" www.allaboutsikhs.com/mansukh/042.htm.

Allied Irish Bank, "Gurdwara Sri Guru Singh Sabha," *Allied Irish Bank (GB) Business Portal: Feature,* June 28, 2004. www.aibgb.co.uk.

Tribune India, "Bans and Turbans: A Matter of Honour," February 1, 2004. www.tribuneindia.com/2004/20040201/spectrum/mainl.htm.

BBC News/South Asia, "India Set for New Prime Minister," June 9, 2004. newsvote.bbc.co.uk/south_asia.stm.

Sandeep Singh Brar, "Century of Struggle and Success: The Sikh Canadian Experience, Part V, Wartime Contributions," *Sikhism.* www.sikhs.org/100th/part5a.html.

———, "The Fifth Master," Sikhism. www.sikhs.org/guru5.htm.

———, "The First Master: Guru Nanak Dev (1469–1539), *Sikhism.* www.sikhs.org/guru1.htm.

———, "The Fourth Master: Guru Ram Das (1534–1581), *Sikhism.* www.sikhs.org/guru4.htm.

———, "The Khalsa," *Sikhism*. www.sikhs. org/khalsa.htm.

———, "The Tenth Master," Sikhism. www.sikhs.org/guru10.htm.

———, "The Third Master: Guru Amar Das (1479–1574), *Sikhism*. www.sikhs. org/guru3.htm.

———, "A Tribute to the Sikh Contributions in World War I on the Battlefield of France and Belgium," *Sikhism*. www.sikhs.org/www1.

Dominic Casciana, "British Sikhs Find Voice in Political Party," September 13, 2003. *BBC News*. newsvote.bbc.co.uk.

Mike Fox, "Sikh Wins Right to Wear Dagger," May 18, 2002. *BBC News*. news.bbc.co.uk.

Sam Matthews, "Sikh Youngsters Are 'Turning Away from Their Culture,'" *ic Berkshire.co.uk*, January 2, 2004. icberkshire.icnetwork.co.uk.

Nandini Raghavendra, "NRI Doc Makes a Trademark," Times News Network, *Economic Times Online*, January 4, 2004. economictimes.indiatimes.com.

Yonat Shimron, "Sikh(ing) Challenges," *Sikhism*. www.sikhs.org.uk/challenge. htm.

SikhNetwork, "Sikh Americans Encouraged to Contact Senators to Support 'Workplace Religious Freedom Act,'" June 18, 2004. www.sikhnet.com.

Jasjit Singh, "On Being a Sikh," *Sikhism*. www.sikhs.org/art7.htm.

Jaswinder Singh, "My Thirteen Reasons for Sikhism," *Sikhism*. www.sikhs.org/art4. htm.

———, "Why Sikhism?" *Sikhism*. www. sikhs.org/art3.htm.

Amir Tuteja, "Use of English in Gurdwaras," *Sikhism*. www.sikhs.org/art6.htm.

Index

Picture Credits

Cover: MONEY SHARMA/EPA/
  Landov
AFP/Getty Images, 52
© Archivo Iconographico S.A./
  CORBIS, 55
Associated Press/AP, 31, 90, 94, 96
© Kapoor Baldev/Sygma/CORBIS, 87
© Annie Griffiths Belt/CORBIS, 86,
  100
© Bettmann/CORBIS, 56, 60, 81
© Renee C. Byer/Sacramento
  Bee/ZUMA/
  CORBIS, 113
Corel, 7, 12
© Bennett Dean; Eye Ubiquitos/
  CORBIS, 28
© Shelley Gazin/CORBIS, 72
Getty Images, 109
Tim Graham/Getty Images
© Lyndsay Hebberd/CORBIS, 15
© Dave G. Houser/CORBIS, 106

Hulton Archive/Getty Images, 49
© Hulton-Deutsch Collection/CORBIS,
  68, 75
© Kamal Kishore/Reuters/CORBIS, 46,
  103
© Jacques Langevin/CORBIS SYGMA,
  93
© Charles and Josette Lenars/CORBIS,
  71
© Chris Lisle/CORBIS, 42, 44
Lonely Planet Images, 23, 67
© Buddy Mays/CORBIS, 110
National Geographic/Getty Images, 37
© Michael Nicholson/CORBIS, 51
Reuters/Landov, 63
Suzanne Santianne, 8, 11, 59, 82-83
Munish Sharma/Reuters/Landov, 64
© Sikhphotos.com, 19, 20, 27, 34, 38, 41,
  105
Time Life Pictures/Getty Images, 98
Ajay Verma/Reuters/Landov, 78

About the Author

Nancy Hoffman has written several books, including *Life After Death* and *Fairies* (part of Lucent's Mystery Library series), *Heart Transplants* (part of Lucent's Great Medical Discoveries series), *West Virginia*, *South Carolina*, and *Eleanor Roosevelt and the Arthurdale Experiment*. She lives in Nashville, Tennessee, with her husband Tony and daughters Eva and Chloe.

MELROSE PUBLIC LIBRARY

3 1458 00287 877 8

CHILDREN'S ROOM
MELROSE PUBLIC LIBRARY

W9-AAE-281

DISCARDED

Melrose Public Library

The National World War II Memorial

Ted and Lola Schaefer

Heinemann Library
Chicago, Illinois

J 940.54
Schaefer

25.00

© 2006 Heinemann Library
a division of Reed Elsevier Inc.
Chicago, Illinois

Customer Service 888-454-2279

Visit our website at www.heinemannlibrary.com

All rights reserved. No part of this book may be reproduced or utilized in any form or by any means, electronic or mechanical, including photocopying, recording, or by any information storage and retrieval system, without permission in writing from the publisher.

Designed by Richard Parker and Mike Hogg Design
Illustrations by Jeff Edwards
Originated by Chroma Graphics (Overseas) Pte. Ltd
Printed and bound in China by South China Printing Company

10 09 08 07 06
10 9 8 7 6 5 4 3 2 1

Library of Congress Cataloging-in-Publication Data
Schaefer, A. Ted.
 The National World War II Memorial / Ted and Lola M. Schaefer.
    p. cm. -- (Symbols of freedom)
 Includes index.
 ISBN 1-4034-6658-0 (library binding-hardcover) -- ISBN 1-4034-6667-X (pbk.)
 1. World War II Memorial (Washington, D.C.)--Juvenile literature. I. Schaefer, Lola M., 1950- II. Title. III. Series.
 D836.W37S33 2005
 940.54'6'09753--dc22
                                   2005002044

Acknowledgments
The publishers would like to thank the following for permission to reproduce photographs:
Corbis pp. 27 (Bruce Burkhardt), 8, 10, 9 (Hulton-Deutsch Collection), 11 (Seattle Post-Intelligencer Collection; Museum of History and Industry), 6 (Sygma/Jeffrey Markowitz); Getty Images pp. 13 (AFP/Nicholas Roberts), 24 (News), 12 (News & Sport), 15 (News & Sport/Joe Raedle), 25 (Taxi), 7 (Time & Life Pictures); Jill Birschbach/Harcourt Education Ltd pp. 4, 5, 14, 16, 17, 18, 19, 20, 21, 22, 23, 28, 29.

Cover photograph of the National World War II Memorial reproduced with permission of Jill Birschbach/Harcourt Education Ltd.

In recognition of the National Park Service Rangers who are always present at the memorials, offering general information and interpretative tours. We thank you!

Every effort has been made to contact copyright holders of any material reproduced in this book. Any omissions will be rectified in subsequent printings if notice is given to the publishers.

The publishers and authors have done their best to ensure the accuracy and currency of all the information in this book, however, they can accept no responsibility for any loss, injury, or inconvenience sustained as a result of information or advice contained in the book.

Some words are shown in bold, **like this**. You can find out what they mean by looking in the glossary.

Contents

The National World War II Memorial

The National World War II **Memorial** is in Washington, D.C. It is a large memorial made of stone and **bronze**. Many people visit it every day.

This **memorial** remembers the American people who fought for **freedom** in World War II. Many of them served as soldiers. Everyone helped to win the war.

World War II

World War II was the biggest war in history.
It lasted for six years, from 1939 to 1945.
Fighting took place in countries all around
the world.

Battles were fought on land and with ships on the oceans. In the end the United States and its **allies** won the war.

Fighting Soldiers

More than 16 million men and women were U.S. soldiers in World War II. They fought side by side with soldiers from other countries against the enemy.

Soldiers in war need food, uniforms, and **gear**. The United States sent ships filled with these **supplies** to their soldiers all around the world.

Homefront

Men and women back home worked hard to fill the **supply** ships. Some made uniforms and trucks. Others built airplanes and tanks.

Farmers grew more food. People raised money to help pay for the war. Children collected **scrap metal** for factories. Everyone in the United States worked together.

Building a Memorial

In 1993, the U.S. Congress formed a
commission to plan a National World War II
memorial. They chose Friedrich St. Florian to
design and build it.

St. Florian worked with a **sculptor**, a **landscape artist**, a stonecutter, and others to build the memorial. It was finished and **dedicated** in May 2004.

Welcome to the Memorial

Two U.S. flags welcome visitors to the National World War II **Memorial**. The flagpoles have stone bases covered with the service seals of the U.S. **military** forces.

Stone ramps and steps lead into the memorial past benches and grass. Along each side are two **granite** walls. Each wall holds twelve large panels.

The Panels

The panels are **bronze sculptures** set into the walls. They are pictures that tell the story of the United States during World War II.

Many panels show U.S. soldiers fighting on land, in the air, and at sea. Here women and men are working in an airplane factory during the war.

The Pillars

Past the panels, the **memorial** gets bigger. In
the middle is a long pool. Around the pool
are 56 stone pillars in two curved rows.

WYOMING

WASHINGTON

SOUTH DAKOTA

Each pillar stands for a state or **territory** of the United States. They are joined together with **bronze** ropes. This shows the **unity** of the country.

The Pavilions

A tall **pavilion** reaches up from the center of each row of pillars. Inside each pavilion are four **columns** holding **bronze** eagles.

A bronze medal is set into the floor of each pavilion. Around it are the words, "**Victory** on land, victory at sea, and victory in the air."

The Freedom Wall

The fight for **freedom** was very costly. Many American soldiers died in World War II. These brave soldiers are remembered on the Freedom Wall.

HERE WE MARK THE PRICE OF FREEDOM

The Freedom Wall curves along one side of the **memorial**. It is covered with 4,000 gold stars. Each star stands for 100 soldiers who died in the war.

Remembering Great Americans

The Americans who fought in World War II did great things. They worked hard and made the United States strong. The war for **freedom** was won.

The **victory** in World War II made life better for people around the world. They lived in peace without fear.

Visiting the Memorial

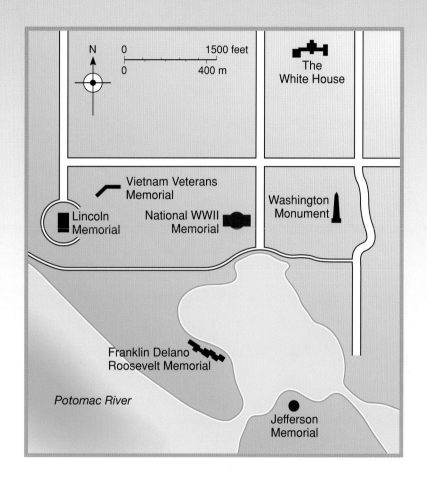

Here is a map showing the National World War II **Memorial** on the **National Mall**. It is between the Lincoln Memorial and the Washington Monument.

When you visit the memorial, remember the people who worked together during World War II. They helped save **freedom** around the world. They were great Americans.

Fact File

National WWII Memorial

★ During World War II, families put blue stars in their windows to show they had a family member serving in the **military** forces. A gold star showed that a family member had died in the war.

★ The site of the National World War II **Memorial** was **dedicated** in 1995. Soil from fourteen overseas World War II cemeteries was brought to Washington, D.C. and sprinkled on the building site.

★ Over 400 **design** ideas were sent to the memorial **commission**. Everyone thought that the design of Friedrich St. Florian was the best!

★ The National World War II Memorial cost $195 million. Many different people gave this money. It is the largest and most expensive memorial in Washington, D.C.

Timeline

National WWII Memorial

★ 1939   World War II begins in Europe

★ 1941   The United States joins World War II

★ 1945   On May 8 World War II in Europe ends
                     On August 14 the war in the Pacific ends

★ 1993   The National World War II Memorial
                     Commission is set up

★ 1995   The memorial site is dedicated

★ 1996   Friedrich St. Florian's design is chosen for the
                     memorial

★ 2000   On Veterans Day, work starts on the memorial

★ 2004   The National World War II Memorial is
                     finished and dedicated

Glossary

allies friend or partner, especially in wartime

battle fight between two armies

bronze hard, reddish brown metal that is a mixture of copper and tin

column tall, upright pillar that helps hold up a building or statue

commission group of people who meet to do a certain task or job

dedicate have a ceremony that opens a new bridge, hospital, or memorial

design draw the shape and style of something

freedom having the right to say, behave, or move around as you please

gear equipment, tools, and supplies

granite hard rock often used as a building material

landscape artist person who is skilled at using the land and plants to make beautiful outdoor scenes

memorial something that is built to help people remember a person or an event

military having to do with soldiers, the armed forces, or war

National Mall large, park-like area of land in Washington, D.C. where museums and memorials are built

pavilion open building that is used for show

scrap metal metals, such as iron or steel, that are not needed and can be melted and used again

sculptor person who carves shapes out of stone, wood, metal, marble, or clay

supplies food, materials, or tools

territory region, or part, of a country that is not a state or province

unity parts joined together to make a stronger whole

victory win in a contest, battle, or war

More Books to Read

An older reader can help you with these books:

Britton, Tamara. *World War II Memorial*. Edina, Minn.: ABDO, 2005.

Hargrove, Julia. *National World War II Memorial: Historic Monuments*. Carthage, Ill.: Teaching & Learning Company, 2002.

Visiting the Memorial

The National World War II Memorial is open every day of the year, except Christmas Day (December 25), 8:30 A.M. to midnight. Park rangers are present during these times to answer questions or give talks on the memorial.

To ask for a brochure and map of the National World War II Memorial, write to this address:

National Park Service
900 Ohio Drive SW
Washington, D.C. 20024.

Index